ADMINISTRATIVE AND EXECUTIVE ASSISTANT
CAREER STARTER

ADMINISTRATIVE AND EXECUTIVE ASSISTANT

career starter

2nd edition

Shirley Tarbell

with Lauren B. Starkey

LearningExpress

New York

Copyright © 2002 LearningExpress, LLC.

All rights reserved under International and Pan-American Copyright Conventions.
Published in the United States by LearningExpress, LLC, New York.

Library of Congress Cataloging-in-Publication Data
Tarbell, Shirley.
    Administrative and executive assistant career starter : finding and getting a
great job / by Shirley Tarbell with Lauren B. Starkey.
    p. cm.
    ISBN 1-57685-396-9 (pbk.)
    1. Administrative assistants—Vocational guidance. 2. Secretaries—
Vocational guidance. 3. Career development. I. Starkey, Lauren B., 1962–
II. Title.
    HG5547.5 .T388 2002
    651.3'023'73—dc21   2001050788

Printed in the United States of America
9 8 7 6 5 4 3 2 1
Second Edition

ISBN 1-57685-396-9

For more information or to place an order, contact LearningExpress at:
    900 Broadway
    Suite 604
    New York, NY 10003

Or visit us at:
    www.learnatest.com

Contents

Contents

Introduction

Why Become an Administrative or Executive Assistant?

Administrative assistants are in demand in almost every industry—from corporations to hospitals, Internet start-ups to retail operations. Check the help wanted ads in any newspaper, and you will find a wide variety of jobs available, with pay ranging anywhere from the low teens to six figures. But the opportunities for employment aren't the only exciting aspect of this field.

Administrative assistants routinely use the most advanced computer software, including word processing, database, desktop publishing, and graphics programs. Your knowledge of these systems will help determine where you land a job, and how far you rise up through the ranks once you're employed.

You can begin working as an administrative assistant as quickly or as slowly as you want. Some enter the field after graduation from high school, while others pursue a six-month to one-year certificate program, one-year diploma program, two-year associate degree, or four-year bachelor's degree. Whichever you choose, you will stand an excellent chance of getting a good job when you finish school. This book will give you the knowledge to select the type of training that's right for you.

Chapter	*Description*
One	In this chapter, you will explore the field. You will find out what
The New Face of Secretarial	an administrative assistant is and does. You will also learn
Work: Choosing a Career as	about hiring trends, find sample job descriptions and salaries,
an Administrative Assistant	and read what some current administrative assistants think
	about the job.

Two
Getting the Education
You Need

This chapter will explain the importance of training, and how to decide what kind of training is right for you. It explains the different types of programs and how to succeed once you've entered one. You will also see sample courses and tuition costs from schools across the country.

Three
Financing Your Education

In this chapter, you will learn the possibilities for financing your education, including loans, scholarships, and grants. The differences between each option are explored, including eligibility, the application process, and how awards are given. The forms you need, where to get them, how to fill them out, and where to send them, are included, and you will also get some tips for simplifying and surviving the process.

Four
Finding Your First Job

This chapter covers the job search process, beginning with a discussion about determining the type of job you really want. There is information on the ten best ways to find employment, from classified ads to networking to Internet resources.

Five
Job Search Skills

In this chapter, you will learn how to hone your job search skills. We show you how to craft winning resumes and cover letters that really get noticed. And once you're noticed and are invited for an interview, you will see how to handle the experience with more polish and less anxiety. Finally, you will learn how to evaluate the job offers you're sure to receive.

Six
Succeeding on the Job

This chapter offers advice on succeeding in your new position. It shows how to manage relationships with your boss and co-workers, as well as your time on and off the job. You will learn about fitting into the particular culture of your new workplace, how to find a mentor, and how to promote yourself to get ahead.

In addition, throughout the book, you will find insights and advice from current and past administrative assistants. Some of these individuals have chosen administration and support as their career, while others have used the job of administrative assistant to get their foot in the door in their industry of choice. No matter what your ultimate career ambition is, this book will help you get started on the path to career success.

The appendices at the end of the book include helpful resources: a list of professional associations, accrediting agencies, and state financial aid offices, as well as a list of training programs, organized by state. Also included are books and periodicals you can refer to for additional information.

So turn the page and begin. This book will give you a head start into the world of work, and remember, the skills you learn and use daily as an administrative assistant will always be there to support you as you grow in your career.

ADMINISTRATIVE AND EXECUTIVE ASSISTANT
CAREER STARTER

CHAPTER one

THE NEW FACE OF SECRETARIAL WORK: CHOOSING A CAREER AS AN ADMINISTRATIVE ASSISTANT

IN THIS chapter, you will get an overview of the administrative assistant field, sometimes referred to as the secretarial field. You will learn what makes a successful administrative assistant, what administrative assistants do, and where they work. Many descriptions of areas of specialization, including legal, medical, and technical, are included. You will also hear advice from a number of individuals already working in the field. Finally, the specific strengths and skills necessary to become a successful administrative assistant will be revealed, along with a blueprint for success as you embark on your career.

IF YOU scan the classified ads in your local paper, you will notice that some companies advertise for secretaries, while others look for administrative assistants. After reading the job descriptions, you may not be sure why they use different titles—the jobs sound the same. For many years, the only acceptable term was *secretary*. It described an office professional who supported her boss mainly by answering the phones, typing, taking dictation, and filing. She acquired her skills at places such as the Executive Secretarial School, Katherine Gibbs, or even her local high school. She might have joined an organization such as the National Secretaries Association or the National Association of Executive Secretaries, and, as a member, been supported with a network of services.

Within the past 20 years, members of those organizations began reporting that their tasks and job responsibilities were increasing. They also noted that the title *administrative assistant* was being used more frequently to describe their jobs. By the late 1990s, many of the schools and organizations for secretaries began to follow suit. The Executive Secretarial School became the ESS College for Business, and Professional Secretaries International became the International Association of Administrative Professionals.

The shift in title reflects a number of changes, including recognition by employers that the role of the secretary was evolving from a strictly supportive one to something more independent. The following table, based on a survey done by Professional Secretaries International, indicates the increase in job responsibilities that go along with the new titles:

Responsibilities	Percentage (if known) 1992	Percentage 1997
Creating spreadsheets	72.9%	89.2%
Creating presentation graphics	40.5%	73.1%
Doing desktop publishing	18.9%	30.3%
Composing correspondence		86.9%
Recommending or making purchasing decisions		78.0%
Handling travel arrangements		55.5%
Training others		48.5%
Supervising others		32.9%
Changes in secretarial duties, 1992–1997		

Source: Professional Secretaries International press release, 1997.

WHAT IS AN ADMINISTRATIVE ASSISTANT?

According to the International Association of Administrative Professionals, an administrative assistant is an "individual who possesses a mastery of office skills, demonstrates the ability to assume responsibility without direct supervision, exercises initiative and judgment, and makes decisions within the scope of assigned authority." Next, each of these areas will be considered in depth to get a clearer picture of the job.

In order for an administrative assistant to possess a mastery of office skills, she must be schooled in the basics, such as keyboarding, dictation, and transcription. In addition, she must know the very latest in office technology. Most places of business rely heavily on e-mail, the Internet, and office software such as Microsoft Word, PowerPoint, Excel, and Lotus. Administrative assistants need to be able to use this technology with proficiency, and keep up with the rapid changes as software improves and new technologies enter the market. Thus, continuing education, whether offered on the job, taken on one's own time over the Internet, or at a community college, is critical.

Administrative assistants need to assume responsibility without direct supervision. This area is one that has changed greatly over the years. Whereas once a secretary answered to her boss in a strictly supportive role —answering the phone, typing up dictated letters, and filing papers—she now may be responsible for calling business associates to provide information or set up meetings, writing correspondence, and creating spreadsheets. Many businesspeople now look to administrative assistants to provide the knowledge and skills necessary for navigating office technology, and shouldering some of the responsibilities once demanded of management.

Exercising initiative and judgment goes hand in hand with making decisions within the scope of assigned authority. Today's administrative assistant needs to be able to think on her feet, often anticipating the next step. Her boss may ask for graphics of the latest sales figures, which he will then share with the regional sales managers. The administrative assistant may take the next step—setting up a teleconference with the managers without being asked. She might also draft correspondence to those managers outlining the sales figures and alerting them to the upcoming conference.

More than ever, administrative assistants are being asked to provide technological know-how and experience, becoming more vital members of their office environments. They are taking on greater responsibility, often working independently and making their own decisions. Administrative assistants' career choices are becoming broader as a result of their knowledge and expertise—there are great opportunities for fulfilling work in exciting, growing industries, such as technology, medicine, and the law.

WHAT DOES AN ADMINISTRATIVE ASSISTANT DO?

Administrative assistant or secretarial duties cover a broad range, depending greatly on level of experience and place of employment. For instance, the job description for a legal secretary is quite different from that of an administrative assistant who works for a computer software company. However, both positions have many tasks in common. The typical duties of a new administrative or executive assistant are:

▶ greet clients, customers, or patients and direct them to the correct person or office
▶ answer the telephone and direct calls to the proper person
▶ make appointments
▶ use a personal computer (the typewriter is all but obsolete in secretarial work today) to type correspondence and reports from a Dictaphone or handwritten copy or type forms
▶ distribute mail

The tasks of a general administrative or executive assistant who advances to, or is hired at, a higher level may also be responsible for:

▶ opening and distributing mail, including personal correspondence
▶ organizing and maintaining files
▶ operating fax machines, photocopiers, and telephones with voice mail capabilities
▶ scheduling appointments
▶ ordering supplies
▶ composing as well as transcribing letters
▶ demonstrating familiarity with a greater variety of computer programs
▶ working with spreadsheet software (the electronic version of an accountant's columnar ledger, pencil, and calculator for bookkeeping and budgeting, tracking sales, preparing financial statements, and analyzing financial problems)
▶ using database management, desktop publishing, and graphics computer programs

▶ making travel arrangements for the boss or being a full-time travel secretary for a number of executives (researching timetables and fares for airlines, hotels, and tour and travel agencies, on the computer or by telephone)

▶ giving information to callers about the company or organization—and knowing when not to

▶ contacting and dealing with clients

▶ arranging conference calls

▶ transcribing—and in some cases creating—the department or company newsletter

A senior-level executive assistant or secretary may (in addition to many of the tasks of a general administrative assistant or secretary):

▶ do highly specialized work that requires knowledge of technical terminology and procedures

▶ conduct research

▶ prepare statistical reports

▶ train and supervise other clerical staff

A subtype of the executive administrative assistant or secretary, the corporate administrative assistant or secretary may:

▶ work directly for the president or chief executive officer (CEO) of a corporation and report to the board of directors

▶ organize corporate meetings and take minutes at those meetings

▶ deal with stockholders

▶ keep a record of stocks and bonds activities

▶ be responsible for certain aspects of corporate records and reports

▶ do light bookkeeping

▶ sometimes travel with the boss to meetings in other cities

No matter what type of administrative assistant position you land, you can expect your responsibilities to grow and change over time. There is consensus among experts—from the Bureau of Labor Statistics to officials of secretarial schools—that increasing automation will continue to transform the nature of administrative assistant/secretarial work. The administrative assistant or secretary has already been freed from many routine tasks, such as tedious retyping of letters the boss has revised or formatting periodic reports and tables anew each time, by computers. He can now spend time on more responsible and creative tasks, such as setting up and conducting meetings with clients or customers, composing letters and reports as well as transcribing them, doing desktop publishing and creating presentation graphics, and setting up databases.

As the profession continues to evolve, you will be presented with more and more opportunities for growth within your career. Whether you take on more responsibility within a job or leave your job for a new one in another type of business, you will be in charge of your own professional destiny. As the demand for skilled administrative assistants remains steady throughout the country, it can even provide you with the opportunity to move to a new area—and almost guarantee that you will be able to find a job.

WHAT MAKES A GREAT ADMINISTRATIVE ASSISTANT?

At the beginning of this chapter, a number of attributes required of a successful administrative assistant were mentioned. In addition to technical skill and a willingness to take on responsibility, there are a number of less tangible attributes that help spell success in the field. The latter might be considered even more important than the technical know-how, because they can't be taught in school. Deborah Conger, who was once a secretary and is now the elected county recorder of Johnson County, Iowa, says an ideal administrative assistant should be:

▶ trustworthy, honest, and ethical
▶ someone who will make me look good, who is supportive of my goals
▶ smart—someone who is not naive and whose opinion I can trust
▶ dependable
▶ accurate
▶ diplomatic and tactful, with good communication skills
▶ someone with a good professional track record
▶ willing to learn, to take instruction, and to follow directions

► flexible
► creative and imaginative, stopping just short of eccentricity, though there are offices in which even eccentricity is a plus
► someone who takes initiative and has the ability to work independently
► talented in getting along with a variety of people

Use this list to assess your own skills and attributes at this time. Are there any items on the list you need to develop or improve? Many of the items deal with a certain mindset (such as possessing a willingness to learn), while others have to do with your values. Determine ways in which you can work toward developing or improving what's lacking. For example, you can begin working toward being dependable long before you enter the job market. Set a goal for yourself, and then take steps to achieve it.

HIRING TRENDS AND SALARIES

According to the Bureau of Labor Statistics, job openings for administrative assistants and secretaries are plentiful, especially in industries experiencing rapid growth, such as technology, medicine, and the law. Although technological advances are replacing some secretarial duties, these same advances are also creating job opportunities. In addition, the Bureau's 2000–2001 report concludes:

> [M]any secretarial job duties are of a personal, interactive nature and, therefore, not easily automated. Duties such as planning conferences, receiving clients, and transmitting staff instructions require tact and communication skills. Because automated equipment cannot substitute for these personal skills, secretaries will continue to play a key role in the office activities of most organizations.

Ray Meyer, director of admissions at the Dallas-based ESS College for Business—a well-known and well-respected ACICS-accredited junior college in operation for over 40 years—points out that with the advent of the computer, the executive administrative assistant or secretary position has expanded to include new duties that are often managerial and says that the technological advances in secretarial work will lead to more, not fewer, jobs for secretaries/administrative assistants. Eleanor Vreeland, a consultant to Katharine Gibbs (a company that operates nine business schools in the eastern United States), asserts that, "although we have moved from typewriters to new technology, someone still has to coordinate all the output, whether that person's title be 'secretary,' 'administrative assistant,' or something else."

According to a salary survey conducted by OfficeTeam (www.officeteam. com), starting administrative assistants earn an average of $21,500 to $26,500. This excludes those specializing in legal or medical work (where many of the new jobs in the field are appearing). The Health Care Job Store's survey of medical administrative assistants reports an average salary of $29,382, while legal secretaries can expect to earn an average of $32,000.

THE IMPORTANCE OF TRAINING

In order to understand and be able to use that technology effectively, you've got to learn, study, and practice. The best place to do that is in a post-secondary training program. Even if you graduate from high school with excellent keyboarding and other office skills, it's unlikely you will get far in your career without some sort of advanced schooling. Not only will you learn and gain proficiency with the latest office software, but you will also get to sample the working world through an internship and get invaluable help with your job search when you're ready to graduate.

Because formal training is so important, two entire chapters of this book have been devoted to the subject of your education and how to pay for it. As you read through Chapter 2, remain flexible regarding your ideas about education. You may think that you should jump into the job market right out of high school (and that may be your course of action after reading this book), but be willing to consider other options. There are many programs that take just months to complete, and they offer many of the benefits that longer programs do.

If you haven't considered education beyond high school because you've always felt you couldn't afford it, Chapter 3 will take you through the financial aid marketplace, explaining the types of aid available, where they can be found, and how and when to apply. However, if you didn't graduate from high school, your first step is to get a General Equivalency Diploma, or GED. You must complete a battery of tests in math, reading, writing, social studies, and science.

To prepare for the GED tests, you may want to sign up for classes or individualized study offered in many communities through adult schools, public libraries, and nonprofit agencies. LearnATest.com offers online practice exams for the GED, and this service also may be offered at your local library, free of charge. Public television series often offer study materials and educational support through phone contact and occasional teacher/student face-to-face meetings on campus. Technical colleges also offer these services and are generally official GED test sites. Some states recognize the life experience of adults who did not graduate from high school but who have learned skills equivalent to those expected of high school graduates. They evaluate and give credit for skills learned on the job, through raising a family, or from one's own self-directed learning. Check with your state's higher education department, listed in Appendix A, for more information about obtaining a GED in your area.

SPECIALIZATION

The administrative assistant field is wide-ranging, covering a large number of very different types of jobs. While a general secretarial course of study will prepare you for much of what you need to know and do on the job (including jobs in specialized areas), you will need additional education for the increased tasks and responsibilities that come with specialized jobs. Some of the most common areas of specialization are detailed in the next section.

Legal

Legal secretaries are employed by law firms, government agencies, financial institutions, and insurance companies to handle the administrative duties generated by legal actions. Administrative assistants interested in this specialization should receive training in the law as it pertains to their field, in addition to general secretarial training. Knowledge of legal terminology, ability to prepare legal documents, and skill in performing legal research are all attributes that will help land a job with a law firm or other employer.

You can become a specialist in this area by taking courses, and even receiving a specialized certificate or degree. However, some law firms do hire generalists, and train them on the job. Clinton Community College, a branch of the State University of New York, offers a Legal Office Assistant certificate to students who complete a curriculum that includes the following courses:

Legal Office Procedures and Terminology
Business Law I
Principles of Accounting
Business Practicum
Advanced Information Processing

While job descriptions vary based on place of employment and type(s) of law practiced by the employer, legal secretaries commonly:

- ▶ edit and process legal documents, such as contracts and court papers
- ▶ rely on legal reference books, standard form manuals, and case files
- ▶ use computers, typewriters, and word processing equipment to edit legal forms and documents
- ▶ file papers with the courts, government agencies, and other interested parties
- ▶ keep track of actions taken, deadlines for future filings, and scheduled court appearances
- ▶ remind attorneys about upcoming events or appointments and any needed preparations
- ▶ keep a record of services rendered, time, or money spent on cases by the attorney or other staff members
- ▶ greet clients and answer telephone calls
- ▶ make appointments and travel arrangements for attorneys and staff

For more information, check with one of the national associations for legal secretaries, listed in Appendix A. You may also want to search the Internet with the terms "legal secretary and education" to see the types of training programs available.

Medical

Medical administrative assistants or secretaries work in single- or multi-physician medical offices, and large health care organizations such as hospitals, clinics, and insurance companies. In addition to general secretarial skills, those interested in pursuing this work should have specialized training in medical ethics, medical terminology, anatomy, health insurance and billing, medical transcription, and word processing.

The title "medical assistant" is more frequently being used now to describe an employee who assists with administrative and, sometimes, clinical duties. While often used interchangeably with medical secretary, the job of medical assistant can be mostly clinical in nature. This depends upon the place of employment and training obtained by the employee. Some medical assistant training programs cover both areas, offering classes in secretarial and administrative skills, as well as in physician assistance (for instance, taking blood pressure, collecting lab specimens, and sterilizing medical supplies). When looking for a training program, or a job, be sure to understand fully the scope of the program or offer of employment (especially if you're not interested in the clinical side of the job).

Typical duties of a medical secretary include:

▶ transcribing dictation and preparing correspondence for physicians or dentists
▶ assisting physicians or medical scientists with reports, speeches, articles, and conference proceedings
▶ recording simple medical histories directly from patients
▶ arranging for patients to be hospitalized

As with legal secretaries, medical secretaries can receive training on the job, or attend a degree or certificate program to get the skills and knowledge necessary. Northeast State Community College in Tennessee offers a two-year certificate program in Medical Office Technology, which teaches basics such as transcription, records management, and word processing. The program also includes the following courses:

Medical Terminology
Fundamentals of Insurance Claims and Patient Billing
Medical Office Procedures

Technical

A technical administrative assistant or secretary works for scientists or engineers in technical, research, and academic settings. In addition to strong general secretarial skills, someone wishing to specialize in this area should have experience typing specialized technical material, and be a computer specialist. Some employers expect proficiency in the use of HTML, while others may seek a Macintosh expert or Webmaster. A working knowledge of specific computer software, such as PlainTeX, AmsteX, and LateX is also helpful, as the material to be keyboarded may contain a substantial amount of complex mathematical formulae and equations.

There are no specific training programs designed to prepare an administrative assistant to work in this specialty. Training may be obtained on the job, and through advanced computer courses. A background in science and/or engineering is also helpful. One way to get the education needed to be a technical assistant is to attend a college or university, and take courses in science and engineering, computers, business, and management. General secretarial skills could be learned from an online course, or another option as described in Chapter 2.

Typical duties of a technical administrative assistant include:

▶ preparing correspondence, budgets, curriculum vitae, annual reports, and special exams
▶ maintaining the technical library
▶ providing graphic design services
▶ creating and maintaining databases

▶ gathering and editing materials for scientific papers

▶ formatting and entering information on employer's Web pages

▶ typing technical research manuscripts, specialized tables, proposals, and monographs

WHERE DO ADMINISTRATIVE ASSISTANTS WORK?

Once you enter the workforce, your overall job satisfaction will depend largely on how well you like the office environment of your employer. Therefore, it is critical that you give consideration not only to the type of job you would like to have, but where you would like to work. There are big differences between corporations and small, family-owned companies, between large, glamorous department stores and auto parts stores.

Since administrative assistants/secretaries are needed in hospitals, churches, charitable institutions, and in such diverse businesses as auto body shops, riding stables, bakeries, day spas, and funeral homes, it's impossible to summarize every work environment. Even the size of a company or institution is not necessarily an indication of its level of formality or rigidity of rules. A small law office can be more formal, for example, than an office in a large advertising agency or one in a giant university. And a huge corporation that got its start outside the mainstream—such as Celestial Seasonings or Microsoft—can be extremely informal.

Next is a general outline of workplaces, including advantages and disadvantages of each. Also included are recent job advertisements for positions in these various workplaces. As you read the descriptions below, keep in mind your reactions to each. You may already have a good idea as to the type of setting you prefer. For more information about different workplace cultures, see Chapter 6.

Corporations and Large Businesses

Corporations are, because of their size, hierarchical. You will find in these organizations that there are often senior-level managers, who supervise junior-level managers, who supervise a staff of support personnel (or another similar hierarchy). There are advantages and disadvantages to working in such a setting. To begin with, you will be presented with a clear path for your career, including possibilities for raises and promotions. An entry-level secretary may be assigned to receptionist or data entry work, and then be moved slowly up through the ranks, gradually adding more tasks with greater responsibilities.

Corporations have many resources that smaller companies don't, so they can offer more to their employees. If you are interested in continuing your education, you may find that your employer will pay some or all of the cost associated with of attending seminars, preparing for certification exams (see the section later in this chapter on certification), or obtaining a college degree. You may also find that working for a corporation will provide:

- ▶ a higher salary
- ▶ better benefits—more days of sick leave and vacation, superior insurance and retirement programs
- ▶ greater opportunity for advancement if the hierarchy is not too rigid—at any rate, greater opportunity within your category
- ▶ more departments to transfer to if the one you're in doesn't suit you
- ▶ better equipment, so your job will be easier and you can be more creative

On the downside, some people feel suffocated by the hierarchy of corporations. Your job description will be very clear, and there will most likely be little opportunity to stray from it. Free-spirited types may find it difficult to fit into the corporate culture, which is typically conservative and somewhat formal. Other drawbacks can include:

- ▶ a more conservative set of rules
- ▶ less variety in the work because of the large, usually specialized work force
- ▶ sometimes less chance for advancement, if the hierarchy is extremely rigid
- ▶ a more impersonal atmosphere
- ▶ the need to spend more money on clothing

Sample Job Advertisements

New York: a top ten public relations firm is seeking an Administrative Assistant for the Executive Assistant to the Chairman.

Primary responsibilities include:

- Providing clerical, administrative, and general office support to the Chairman and Executive Assistant, including word processing, faxing, copying, filing
- Telephones; coordinating international conference calls; answering and screening telephone calls for Chairman and Executive Assistant
- Coordinating and scheduling meetings (internal and external), catering, conference rooms and equipment
- Ability to handle complex travel arrangements (both domestic and international)
- Ability to exercise tact, courtesy, and discretion interacting with staff, clients, and potential clients
- Providing backup relief to the Executive Assistant as needed

Qualifications include:

- High school diploma required; BA/BS preferred
- Minimum two (2) years related administrative experience required
- Ability to balance and successfully resolve often conflicting demands and priorities
- Proficiency in MS Word, Excel, Outlook req.; PowerPoint a plus
- Able to work 9–6, occasional overtime as needed

Salary and Benefits:

- Starting at $46,000; benefits include medical and dental, profit sharing, pension fund, and two weeks' paid vacation the first year

Chicago: a global consulting firm's Human Resources Operations Consulting (HROC) Practice is in need of a highly professional Administrative Assistant.

This individual will provide administrative support to several members of the Practice and should possess the following job requirements:

- 4–5 years of administrative support experience
- Competent use of Microsoft Office Suite for Windows is essential
- Strong team player with excellent verbal and writing skills
- Ability to prioritize multiple projects and adjust workload with frequent interruptions
- Well-organized, diplomatic, and able to work competently under pressure
- Self-starter with ability to work with little supervision
- Flexibility to work overtime

We offer a highly competitive salary along with an excellent benefits package which includes generous time off, short and long term disability insurance, employer paid life insurance, employer funded pension plan, various investment plans, tuition reimbursement along with a choice of 5 health plans and 2 dental plans.

Mid-Sized and Small Companies

Working for a smaller company can bring a number of advantages over a working for a larger one. They include a more relaxed work atmosphere, the chance to take on more interesting assignments not necessarily in your job description, and greater chance for advancement. In addition, you may find a personal, less formal setting in which casual dress is accepted every day and individuals are respected for their unique qualities. Smaller companies tend toward a team-like atmosphere. If one person is successful, everyone shares the success. You will find in such a company a pleasant working environment that promotes growth and cooperation.

However, you may also find lower pay, fewer benefits, and less than state-of-the-art technology. In some very small companies, there is less of a chance for advancement simply because there aren't enough job openings to move up into. In addition, there could be less job stability, as smaller companies fight to stay afloat in economic downturns that might be weathered more easily by large firms. Many are willing to put up with the disadvantages, though, as a trade-off for the many advantages.

Sample Job Advertisements

Small but growing computer software company in San Diego is looking for an administrative assistant who has excellent communication skills, is able to type at least 50 wpm, and has intermediate to advanced knowledge of computer software. Responsibilities will include scheduling appointments, making travel and meeting arrangements, as well as directing phone calls and generating reports daily.

Job Experience: Multi-Line Phone, MS Word, MS PowerPoint, MS Excel
Salary: $22,000 to $27,000 per year

Job Description:

Terrific opportunity for a professional individual ready to move ahead in a great career. As an administrative assistant for this stable, family-oriented commercial insurance company, you will be responsible for supporting the worker's compensation claims department. Quick learning team player with strong computer skills and attention to detail who can work well with minimum supervision. Rewarding work environment that offers business casual dress attire, friendly and professional coworkers, and a gym and cafeteria on premises.

Job Experience:

Access, data entry, general office, typing, Microsoft Excel, Microsoft Word, Quality Assurance, Ten Key by Touch

Salary:

$10.00 to $11.00 per hour

Nontraditional or Entrepreneurial Offices

This category cuts across the others above, as entrepreneurial businesses can be large or small. What they have in common is an atmosphere that emphasizes risk-taking and working independently. Employees tend to wear many hats and are given a wide range of responsibilities. These businesses can be very competitive; they are frequently in quick, big-money fields, and they reward those who help them gain advantages over the competition. Their advantages over traditional offices of any size can include:

- ▶ less emphasis on job title; more emphasis on individual
- ▶ greater opportunity to move up
- ▶ greater flexibility of work rules
- ▶ greater opportunity for creativity
- ▶ a more relaxed atmosphere
- ▶ generally a less rigid dress code

Drawbacks can include:

- ▶ lower pay
- ▶ fewer (or no) benefits
- ▶ less job security

Sample Job Advertisements

Growing creative agency in the Minneapolis warehouse district seeks special assistant(s) that can multi-task special projects, provide travel arrangement, coordinate in-house catering, and handle phones and general office operations. This person will help preserve the heart of our organization. It requires they be committed, inventive, thoughtful, resourceful, and enjoy challenges in a unique, fast-paced environment. Work with great people that produce cool stuff! Send cover letter with resume and salary history. We will consider a job share or flex time situation for the right fit.

Qualifications:

Experience in Word, Excel, and PowerPoint a plus

Must be detailed and results-oriented

Ability to make customers, vendors, or colleagues feel comfortable and important

Salary: $11.00 to $13.00 per hour

Louisiana biotechnology firm seeks administrative assistant to grow with us! We just opened our doors last month, and need someone to:

- Provide administrative support to group leaders, project leaders, and research scientists
- Be a partner with the team in pursuing strategic business objectives, including planning, anticipating and managing schedules and activities with an understanding of business priorities
- Provide effective project management support and ensure project outcomes meet customer requirements

Primary Responsibilities include:

- Coordinate/manage daily work processes, calendar(s), internal/external meetings/seminars, travel arrangements, and expense reports
- Coordinate the preparation and handling of incoming/outgoing electronic and written communications, regulatory documents, and presentations
- Provide purchasing support to include requisitions, capital purchases, and retirement of equipment
- Maintain office supplies and equipment
- Act as an information resource
- Participate in special projects and ad hoc tasks as assigned
- Perform additional duties as requested.

Qualifications include a high school diploma or equivalent, some college and 3+ years work experience supporting multiple people. Excellent business administration experience, adept in computerized environments, and excellent interpersonal, organization, time management, and communication skills. Proficient in Microsoft Office applications, SAP software, QuickExpense; Oracle a plus, but not necessary. Ability to effectively perform in a team environment, manage confidential information, determine the priority/order and methods for completing responsibilities. Ability to manage multiple priorities/projects simultaneously, as well as manage routine work flow and work processes. High level of accuracy, attention to detail, and aptitude for independent decision-making. Ability to handle an ever-changing environment and maintain a positive working attitude.

Salary starts at $11.00/hour, but we anticipate being able to offer full benefits, including profit-sharing, within a year. Bonuses and a raise after six months may also be anticipated.

Government and State Institutions

There are thousands of job opportunities in government at the federal, state, and local levels. They include positions with agencies such as the Department of Justice, the Department of the Interior, the Environmental Protection Agency, the Internal Revenue Service, and the Immigration and Naturalization Service. Many of these agencies have state corollaries, although the names may be different. In addition to all of the departments and agencies, there are court systems, both federal and state. There, you could work in the offices of the district attorney or public defender, for example. Other possibilities include state universities and law enforcement agencies.

These workplaces differ from those in any for-profit business in many ways, and they can offer all sorts of atmospheres. Generally, government or state office jobs (such as those at public universities) offer the following:

▶ good pay
▶ good benefits
▶ job security (though lately downsizing has been happening here too)
▶ a fairly relaxed work atmosphere
▶ good chances for advancement within your job category and even outside it, because of a formal testing system for various kinds of jobs

Drawbacks can include:

▶ a tendency toward a more cumbersome bureaucracy
▶ less efficiency in the workplace, which can be frustrating—usually, again, these offices are nonprofit, so there's not as much incentive to economize with money or time as in a large corporation
▶ good pay, but no chance for great pay

Sample Job Advertisements

Job Location: Sacramento, CA

Job Description: Civil service—county government office seeks a transcriptionist to transcribe reports for the Dept. of Health and Human Services. The position involves professional customer service skills and the ability to interact with social workers. This flexible position offers the opportunity to gain more experience providing a foot in the door for a position with Sacramento County. Job duties required, but not limited to, are typing of at least 50 wpm, good grammar, and Dictaphone experience is a plus. This position also provides the opportunity to work independently.

Job Experience: Customer Service, MS Word, Word Processing

Salary: $10.00 to $11.00 per hour

Employer: Justice Dept., Immigration and Naturalization Service (INS), Milwaukee Metro Area

Position: Administrative Support Assistant (office automation)

Series/Grade: GS-0303-07/

Salary: $29,607.00 TO $38,488.00, annual

Promotion potential: GS-07

Announcement number: CH-DT-1-123062

Remarks: Job applicants must submit a form C to be considered for this position

Temporary Agency Offices

The temporary work force has been cited as the fastest-growing work category in the country. If you want variety and a certain amount of freedom, this work can be appealing. The advantages of temporary over permanent work can include:

▶ the opportunity for a more flexible lifestyle (you aren't stuck in a 52-week-per-year commitment)

▶ a greater variety of kinds of tasks and office atmospheres

▶ no fear of getting trapped in a job you hate

▶ the opportunity to shop around for a permanent job you really like ("temp-to-perm" employment options are becoming more plentiful)

► the opportunity to move from workplace to workplace to find out what kind of office atmosphere is best for you

Drawbacks can include:

► somewhat lower pay, although these days temporary agencies are giving raises
► less (or no) chance for advancement beyond administrative assistant or secretary
► fewer or sometimes no benefits—though this is changing, and many temporary agencies now have benefits
► less job security—in smaller cities and towns, there can be dry spells between jobs

Following Your Interest and Paying the Bills

Byron and Valerie Demmer decided some 15 years ago that they wanted to travel and to live something other than a mainstream life, so they went to work for temporary agencies and love the freedom it gives them. They have lived in California, Colorado, New Mexico, Missouri, Massachusetts, and New York, doing temporary clerical and secretarial work while pursuing their interests in art and philosophy, disciplines that add richness to their lives but don't always pay the bills.

The couple has noticed that in the last few years temporary work is more plentiful than ever, due to the proliferation of temporary agencies. Whereas Kelly Services, Manpower, and a few others were once their main sources of employment, now there are many more agencies to choose from. They like the variety of work and the ability to pick and choose. "If you don't like the job, it's okay—you know you're not stuck," Valerie says. "On the other hand, if you decide you want to settle down, there are a lot of jobs that are 'temporary to permanent.' " This change has occurred in the last ten years, Valerie says. "In the old days, the temporary agencies didn't like it if you took a job with an employer they sent you to. Nowadays, employer and employee can try each other out. If there's a good fit, you can make the position permanent with the blessing of the agency that sent you."

Byron points out that temporary agencies now offer benefits, something that was not done in the past. These benefits include training, and the opportunity to pick up a greater variety of skills than in almost any other clerical occupation. As will be discussed in Chapter 2, many temporary agencies now make computer software and other types of training available to their employees at no charge. Medical and life insurance, pension or 401(k) fund, and paid vacation are other benefits you might receive when working for a temp agency.

Home Offices

Many organizations are now hiring at-home employees for various kinds of administrative work involving computer operations. Working at home is ideal for some, especially if you have obligations that make it inconvenient to leave the house for long periods of time. Opportunities are growing, thanks to businesses that are able to cut costs by using non-salaried workers. They don't have to pay for your office space, equipment, or benefits. Plus, people who work at home have been shown to be more efficient and productive than those who come into the office.

If you choose to work at home, there are two ways to go about it: freelance or working for a company or organization. Freelancers find much of their work on the Internet, where they may advertise their services. They contract each job separately, negotiating their fees and a schedule for when and how the work is to be completed. If you work at home for one company, you will be given a steady workload and may be put on the payroll. It is even possible to find a company that will set you up with a home office, equipped with a computer networked into the main office.

The advantages of working at home include:

- freedom to set your own hours
- greater variety of work (if you freelance)
- freedom from restrictive rules about breaks, length of lunch hours, taking off for appointments, and so forth (if you freelance)
- no office politics
- being able to work in casual clothing

The drawbacks can include:

► less job security (if you freelance)
► few or no benefits (if you freelance)
► lower pay (sometimes)
► cabin fever from staying home too much

To find work-at-home opportunities, search the Internet using keywords such as "administrative assistant and freelance," and look for websites specifically geared to this type of employment, such as 2Work-At-Home.com and www.homeworkersnet.com, that offer job listings and support services for home-based administrative and clerical jobs. Also check the classified ads for companies that are looking for home-based help.

OPPORTUNITIES FOR ADVANCEMENT

In most companies and organizations of moderate or large size, there is chance for advancement. Examples include a move from clerk-typist or receptionist to administrative assistant or secretary, or from a lower-level administrative assistant or secretary to a higher-level one. In order to maximize your chances for a promotion, concentrate on two areas:

1. Learn about the business. Even if you have fairly routine duties, it's wise to learn as much as you can about aspects of the business or organization outside your job description. Find out management's philosophy, about how clients or customers are acquired, and about how products are produced or services provided. Showing interest in the business or organization as a whole is the surest way to advance and to gain the skills to succeed once you do advance. (If you have no interest in what your employer does, it may be time to look for employment elsewhere.)

2. Upgrade your skills, not only those needed for your current job but those needed for a better one. Be sure your office-related skills are first-rate, and work toward acquiring proficiency in other areas as well, such as effective research, writing, and speaking, purchasing,

bookkeeping, and whatever else is relevant to the business or organization as a whole. Especially important is continuing to upgrade your computer skills—computer literacy is an absolute must these days. When you feel you're ready to advance, don't wait for your boss to suggest a promotion. Be proactive about your career by applying for a job with more responsibility and a higher salary, a job working for a higher-level supervisor within your company or organization, or a more challenging job with another firm or organization. Read Chapter 6 for more information about the process of promoting yourself.

There is some controversy about the chance for advancement from administrative assistant to other job titles in a company or organization. In some companies and organizations, you may be put into the category "secretary" and find your special knowledge and expertise ignored. If possible, steer clear of those places, because whether you remain a secretary or not, you won't receive the respect you deserve. There is good potential for advancement in the more enlightened companies and organizations, however.

As current administrative and executive assistants will share with you, with the greater demand for complex skills, especially computer skills, administrative assistant work can be challenging and creative. And you will be able to move to different kinds of work, if you so choose. *The Merriam-Webster Secretarial Handbook* asserts that this is the case, especially for talented individuals in fields such as publishing, fashion design, personnel, television, and newspapers. Small entrepreneurial companies also frequently promote from within, because each person, from lowest to highest rank, tends to wear more than one hat. Additionally, although men are joining the secretarial ranks in greater numbers, this has been a traditionally female field for many years, and increased recognition of women's talents has translated into more advancement opportunities.

If you're ambitious, there are plenty of creative positions and excellent salaries within the administrative assistant category. It's not uncommon to make $40,000 a year, and as already mentioned, $80,000 to $90,000 is possible if you have the drive. Consider advancing into a more interesting industry or to a job with more perks. Working for the CEO of a large corporation or working on the support staff of one of the glamour industries can pay off in other than monetary ways as well.

CERTIFICATION

There are a number of professional certifications available to administrative assistants. Most require job experience before you can take the qualifying exam, but some will substitute a college degree for experience. The possible advantages of obtaining certification include:

▶ distinguishing oneself from the crowd when applying for a job or seeking a promotion
▶ gaining further education through preparation for the exam(s)
▶ receiving a higher salary than those professionals without certification (a recent IAAP Membership Profile study shows that those with a Certified Professional Secretary designation earn an average of $2,228 more per year than those who do not have certification)
▶ demonstrating to your employer that you are a professional, committed to advancing your career
▶ receiving college credit (many colleges and universities offer course credit for passing certification exams)

Certified Professional Secretary (CPS)

The CPS is a one-day, three-part exam offered by the International Association of Administrative Professionals (IAAP). More than 58,000 administrative professionals have achieved the CPS rating since 1951. To take exam, you must be currently employed as an administrative professional, or have two years of experience and a bachelor's degree, three years' experience with an associate degree, or four years' experience with no degree. IAAP charges $160.00, plus a $35.00 processing fee ($60.00 for nonmembers). The certification is valid for a period of five years, at which time one must fulfill a continuing education requirement to keep the CPS designation from lapsing.

To prepare for the exam, you may purchase a study guide from IAAP. If you fail one or more parts of the exam, you may retake that part. The IAAP allows three years to pass all parts of the exam. The content of the exam is as follows:

Part I: Finance and Business Law—30% economics, 35% accounting, 35% business law.
Part II: Office Systems and Administration—50% office technology, 25% office administration, 25% business communication.
Part III: Management—36% behavioral science in business, 19% human resources management, 45% organizations and management.

Certified Administrative Professional (CAP)

This certification was offered by the IAAP for the first time in 2001 for those administrative assistants who wish to distinguish themselves further than the CPS. It has some of the same requirements as the CPS and is also valid for five years. The CAP costs $225.00, plus a processing fee of $35.00 ($60.00 for nonmembers). The first three parts of the four-part CAP exam are the same as the CPS, and do not need to be retaken by those holding current CPS certification. Part IV tests for knowledge of organizational planning, including team skills, strategic planning, and advanced administration.

Accredited Legal Secretary (ALS)

Offered by the National Association of Legal Secretaries (NALS), this is a four-hour, three-part exam. To take it, you must have one year of general office experience, the NALS training course, or an accredited office curriculum course. Material covered on the exam is as follows:

Part 1: Written Communications
Part 2: Office Procedures and Legal Knowledge
Part 3: Ethics, Human Relations, and Judgment

If you fail a part or parts, you may retake them, paying the full exam fee each time ($50.00 for full-time students, $75.00 for NALS members, $100.00 for others). Certification is good for five years; to renew, you must fulfill a continuing education requirement (15 hours of approved education, including postsecondary courses, seminars, and workshops).

Professional Legal Secretary (PLS)

This certification is also offered through the NALS. Any person who has had three years' experience in the legal field may take the examination (membership in NALS is not a requirement). A partial waiver of the three-year legal experience requirement may be granted for postsecondary degrees, successful completion of the ALS exam, or other certifications. The maximum waiver is one year.

To prepare for the exam the NALS has published a resource manual, which is available for sale or by taking a course offered by the association (check their website, or contact them by phone: see Appendix A for contact information). A fee of $150.00 is charged to NALS members; others pay $200.00 to take the exam, which covers:

Part 1: Written Communications
Part 2: Office Procedures and Technology
Part 3: Ethics and Judgment
Part 4: Legal Knowledge and Skills

Certified Legal Secretary Specialist (CL§)

Legal Secretaries International offers this designation in four areas of the law: civil trial, probate, real estate, and business law. Qualifications include a minimum of five years' law-related experience (three years with a four-year degree, PLS, or CLA certification; two years with a two-year degree or ALS certification). There is an examination fee of $25.00.

Material covered on the exams and study resources are as follows:

The Certified Legal Secretary Specialist: Civil Trial Examination consists of three sections: pretrial matters, trial, and posttrial matters. Additional resource materials are: United States Constitution; Federal Rules of Civil Procedure, Appellate Procedure, and Evidence.

The Certified Legal Secretary Specialist: Probate Examination consists of three sections on probate law and procedures. Additional resource is the Uniform Probate Code.

The Certified Legal Secretary Specialist: Real Estate Examination consists of three sections on real estate law and procedures. Resources are listed above.

The Certified Legal Secretary Specialist: Business Law Examination consists of three sections. Resources are listed above, plus the Uniform Commercial Code.

PERSONAL PREFERENCE INVENTORY

You've read about what an administrative assistant is and what one does. You've learned where they work and how they can get ahead. Now you're ready to determine the type of secretarial position that's right for you. This questionnaire was designed to get you thinking about your ideal job, and the many components that work together to create it. Circle the answer that best describes your preference or situation in the questions below:

1. Which do I prefer?
   a. fast-paced work that keeps me busy with multiple tasks all day
   b. a more relaxed job, with enough work to keep me busy and interested, but some time now and then to chat with coworkers
2. Which best fits my chosen lifestyle?
   a. taking time each morning to groom and dress for success
   b. rolling out of bed, showering, throwing something on, and dashing out the door
3. Which of the following best describes my home situation?
   a. I do not have children or anyone else who depends on me on a daily basis.

b. I have children or someone else dependent on me or likely to need my attention at unpredictable times.

4. Which of the following best describes my favorite pastimes?

    a. sports and hobbies in which I interact and compete with others

    b. individual sports or such solitary pastimes as reading, painting, and gardening

5. How important is money to me?

    a. very important, and I'm willing and able to work extra hours to make more

    b. important, but not that important; a satisfying job and a good balance of work, play, and family life rank first

6. In what kind of environment do I do my best work?

    a. one that's structured and deadline oriented

    b. one in which I can work fairly independently with flexible regulations

Take note of your answers. The questionnaire is not an absolute measure of the kind of job you should look for, but in general if you answered **a** to most of the questions, you'd do better in a more structured and faster-paced (maybe even high-powered) office. If you answered **b** to most of them, look for a medium or small office with flexible rules. You might even prefer a zany, entrepreneurial company, or perhaps be happiest with a permanent temporary job with benefits.

In addition to the above questionnaire and what it reveals, ask yourself this question: Which of the following subjects interests me most?

Art	New Age
Environment	Religion
Finance	Science
Law	Sociology
Medicine	Sports

You might have an addition to this list—perhaps an area of interest related to a hobby or other pursuit. Consider this subject as you read through the rest of this book; is there an administrative assistant position or specialty related to it? Your own interests, likes, and dislikes, can help determine the education you pursue, as well as the positions you apply for.

It might be tempting to take the first good position that's offered. It's easy, if you're in school, to let a well-meaning counselor talk you into a particular kind of job because it pays the most or offers stability. But remember that there is great variety in administrative and executive assistant jobs, and you stand a much better chance of succeeding in a position that suits your interests, lifestyle, and temperament.

Read on to learn how to prepare for your career as an administrative assistant. In the next chapters, you will learn how to get the education you need (and how to pay for it), where the jobs are, and how to find and succeed in one.

THE INSIDE TRACK

Who: Michele Williams
What: Staff Associate/Assistant Librarian
Where: USX Corporation

INSIDER'S STORY

I have always liked the fast-paced environment of a busy office. I've been interested in the administrative field ever since I was a little girl, when I would go and visit my mother at work.

I've been in my current position for a year and a half. I do administrative duties, as well as backup work wherever I'm needed in the office. I also assist the librarian. Some of my responsibilities include word processing, using Microsoft Office 2000, filing, composing correspondence, and updating spreadsheets daily.

I have no degree or certificate in the administrative field, though I have years of experience. I've received some on-the-job training, and have also built up a lot of work experience, which helped me attain my current position. Computer skills are a must in this field, but without people skills, you'll have a hard time. It's so important to be able to deal well with other people. I've learned that the administrative staff are some of the most important people in a company. Everything you do affects the company's operation, so precision and attention to detail are important.

I can always count on my managers and coworkers to teach me new things. If we're using a program I'm not familiar with, no one gets angry at me. They just teach me what I need to know. My employer has even offered to pay for me to take some computer classes. I always like to grow, and I think that the skills I've learned here will help me work my way up to a higher position.

CHAPTER two

GETTING THE EDUCATION YOU NEED

In this chapter you will learn why training is important. The different types of educational opportunities available, including sample courses and tuition costs from schools around the country, will be explored. You will learn how to choose a training program by evaluating not only the programs, but your needs as well. Finally, tips on succeeding once you're enrolled, including how to land an internship and how to prepare for exams are covered.

THE FACE of secretarial or support staff work is changing at an unprecedented rate. Years ago, a secretary typed, filed, answered phones, fetched the boss's coffee, and that was pretty much it. A book published in 1965 called *You Can Be an Executive Secretary* lists mandatory skills for the secretary as opening mail, taking and typing dictation, filing, having some knowledge of bookkeeping terms, setting up appointments for your boss, and, of course, making coffee. The book advises, "If [your boss] needs three cups of black coffee at his [*sic*] desk each morning to help him face the rigors of the day, see that he gets it—at the right temperature and precise intensity of black."

Now, everything from the job description to the very name of the profession has changed. As noted in Chapter 1, the title "secretary" is routinely being replaced by the more accurate title "administrative assistant" to reflect the complex nature of the work. Indicative of this change is the evolution of one of the leading organizations for administrative assistants. The group that started in 1942 as the National Secretaries Association, and later became Professional Secretaries International, voted to change its name to the International Association of Administrative Professionals (IAAP) in 1998.

Administrative assistants are not making much coffee these days. In fact, their bosses may look to them for the skills and information they themselves lack. A recent *OfficePro* magazine (the publication of the International Association of Administrative Professionals) article entitled "The Digital Office" noted that administrative assistants are expected to be more "high-tech savvy" than those they work for. Alan Hakimi, principal consultant on the technology side of Microsoft's Consulting Services Group, says that administrative assistants are "very responsible for running our business." The article also points out that during the corporate downsizing that took place in the 1990s, many middle-level managers were let go and administrative assistants took up much of the slack. Thus, their job descriptions expanded and responsibilities increased.

WHY YOU NEED TRAINING

The digital office can't be run by just anyone. In addition to having a working knowledge of computer programs such as Microsoft Word, Excel, Lotus, PowerPoint, and Outlook Express, today's administrative assistant may need to generate spreadsheets, charts, and graphs; do desktop publishing using a variety of graphics and drawing software; prepare graphics for presentation at committee meetings, board meetings, and stockholder meetings; and even create databases. He or she may be called upon to research and write reports; substitute for members of management at important meetings, both in the home office and in distant cities; deal with clients or customers in much more than a reception capacity; organize public events; interview prospective employees; and train and supervise workers once they're hired. These skills are taught in administrative assistant training programs.

A second reason to get formal administrative training is that in school you will learn about the wide variety of job opportunities available to you, and get a broader vision of what's possible. You might find you don't want to work in the traditional corporate world. You might decide the fashion or filmmaking industry, a university department, or a small veterinary clinic is right for you. The variety of courses available in a good school will expand your ideas about what an administrative or executive assistant job can be.

A third advantage of education is the availability of job search and placement services through the school you attend. The job placement office can be a great source for internships (sometimes called "externships") during your schooling, which provide on-the-job training (discussed later in this chapter) and possibly job offers once completed. Many schools offer courses in how to search for a job, and when your schooling is completed, you may find that a number of local employers actively recruit graduates from your program.

Jennifer Bergin, a former student at Casco Bay College in Portland, Maine, cites a fourth advantage. Jennifer participated in an externship at Property Management Services, Inc., in Portland and advises, "You will feel more comfortable on the job if you're caught up on the latest technology and have had some experience working." This echoes a statement by Eleanor Vreeland, former chairman of the prestigious Katharine Gibbs School and now consultant and editorial advisory board member of Katharine Gibbs: "Since people just out of high school are unfamiliar with job searching and with going to a job every day, they need special training in order to know how to dress and behave in an office atmosphere. They need to become familiar with how business communicates."

TYPES OF TRAINING PROGRAMS

There are a number of different options when considering the type of education you want and need. If you'd like to jump right into the job market and have basic skills such as typing, you can sign on with a personnel agency that offers training. Or, enroll at a local community college or proprietary school for a quick course of study, usually three to six months. These and other options are explored in greater detail below.

Short-Term Courses

At most colleges offering associate of arts or associate of applied science degrees (as well as at four-year colleges offering bachelor of arts or bachelor of science degrees), you may take individual courses necessary for the kind of job you want, or brush-up courses if your skills have become rusty. In these short courses you usually don't earn a certificate or diploma, but the courses are valuable nonetheless. Eleanor Vreeland cites classes in business communications, personal development (dress and behavior in the world of work), and computer training as valuable for teaching technical skills and skills in how to succeed in an office environment. Such classes are also a way of finding out what you'd like to do in the future or testing a longer program before committing yourself.

The Six- to Twelve-Month Certificate or Diploma Program

In a six-month or 12-month program, you will obtain a certificate or diploma rather than a degree. The course of study might include intensive training in computer basics, personal development, and business communications but fewer general education courses. For example, at King's College in North Carolina, you can earn an Administrative Assistant diploma in eight months. The diploma will qualify you for initial employment as an administrative assistant, and the courses may be transferable to a degree secretarial program if you want to go on with your training. Tuition for the program totals $6,550.00 for 660 credit hours. Here is their 2001 curriculum, which is typical of short-term certificate curricula elsewhere:

Human Relations in the Workplace
Oral Communication
Essentials of Accounting
Business Communications I
Keyboarding I
Word Processing
Intro. To Database Management
Electronic Spreadsheets

Business Communications II
Keyboarding II
Office Procedures I
Professional Development
Adv. Electronic Spreadsheets
Business Communications III
Document Formatting
Office Procedures II
Concepts of Desktop Publishing
Database Management
Written Communications
Document Production

Source: King's College, www.kingscollege.org.

The Associate of Arts and Associate of Applied Science Degrees

The associate of arts degree is a two-year degree program that also prepares the student to enter the final two years of a four-year program leading to a bachelor's degree. Below is the curriculum for a 70-credit-hour administrative assistant associate degree program in Office Technology from Shawnee Community College in Illinois. Shawnee charges $2,940.00 in tuition for county residents; out-of-state students must pay $18,933.60.

First Year, First Semester:
ENG 124 Technical Communication I or ENG 111 English
    Composition
IMS 122 Document Formatting
IMS 123 Beginning Formatting
IMS 120 Records & Information Management
PSY 224 Practical Psychology or PSY 211 Introduction to Psychology
SEM 111 College Orientation
INT 111 Career Development
Total Hours: 17

First Year, Second Semester:

ENG 221 Technical Communication II or ENG 112 English
   Composition

MAT 121 Technical Mathematics or MAT 210 General Elementary
   Statistics

IMS 125 Business Machines

IMS 223 Document Production

IMS 224 Shorthand/Speedwriting/Trans. II

IMS 117 Telephone Communication

COM 166 Intro. to Lotus 1-2-3 or COM 167 Intro. to Microsoft Excel

Total Hours: 18

Second Year, First Semester:

IMS 227 Office Information Processing I

ACC 111 Accounting *or* BUS 124 Bookkeeping

BUS 214 Business Law

COM 111 Business Computer Systems

IMS 128 Machine Transcription

COM 168 Introduction to Desktop Publishing

Total Hours: 18/17

Second Year, Second Semester:

SPC 210 Interpersonal Communication or SPC 111 Speech

IMS 236 Office Information Processing II

IMS 226 Administrative Support Procedures

BUS 128 Introduction to Management

IMS 115 Proofreading

IMS 192 Executive Sec./Administrative Asst. Internship

Total Hours: 16

Source: Shawnee Community College, www.shawnee.cc.il.us.

Next is a more ambitious, 103-credit-hour program. ESS College for Business (formerly known as the Executive Secretarial School) in Dallas, Texas, confers an associate of applied science degree in office technology.

General Education Courses
College Mathematics

Composition and Rhetoric

Introduction to Economics

Introduction to Ethics, Introduction to Philosophy, or Introduction to Psychology

Introduction to Public Speaking

Required subtotal: 30

Technical Program Courses

Administrative Office Procedure

Advanced Communications

Advanced Computer Applications

Advanced Document Production

Advanced Word Processing

Business Communications

Business Law

Business Management

Business Math

Career Skills

College Accounting

Computer Literacy

Database Management

Desktop Publishing

Developmental English

Document Processing 1

Document Processing 2

Document Processing 3

Document Processing 4

Document Processing 5

Machine Transcription

Spreadsheet Applications

Web Page Design

Word Processing

Source: ESS College for Business, www.esscollege.org.

This ESS College for Business program may be completed in just 13 months. Students attend classes 30 hours a week, rather than the usual 15 to 20 hours at most colleges. Other colleges may allow you to accelerate their associate degree programs if you're willing to put in the extra hours. If this option appeals to you, be sure to ask the school of your choice whether it is available before you make your final decision.

To give you a further idea of the course descriptions for an associate degree, the following courses are a few examples from a typical catalog.

DANVILLE AREA COMMUNITY COLLEGE, DANVILLE, ILLINOIS

Introduction to the Office (fall/spring; three hours)

Emphasizes the fundamentals of word processing, its history, current office practices, organization and structure, workflow, equipment, role of the secretary and management, career opportunities, and basic ten-key instruction.

Professional Secretary Certification I (three hours)

Emphasis given to the behavioral science in business, principles of business law, and governmental controls on business operations.

Desktop Publishing I (fall/spring; three hours)

The fundamentals of layout and design techniques as well as the basic operation of a high-end desktop publishing software program.

Basic Excel (fall/spring; two hours)

An introductory course to develop skills in creating, revising, and printing spreadsheets, charts, and graphs.

Office Systems Internship (as needed; three hours)

On-the-job training in office systems or business-related areas.

Source: Danville Area Community College, www.dacc.cc.il.us.

Specialization

As discussed in Chapter 1, there are a number of specialties within the administrative assistant field. Most schools offer options for specialization within the secretarial and administrative assistant associate degree programs. Some typical options follow (the list is by no means exhaustive).

Administrative assistant/secretary
Administrative assistant/secretary bilingual
Executive administrative assistant/secretary
Medical administrative assistant/secretary

> Legal administrative assistant/secretary
>
> Personnel assistant
>
> Word processing specialist
>
> Desktop publishing
>
> Administrative assistant/secretary with a subspecialty in another field (some possibilities: secondary education, travel and tourism, fashion, film, animal care, insurance, accounting)

In addition to specializing the type of work you would like to do, you can also distinguish yourself by developing a subspecialty (see the last item in the list above). If you're attending a large college or university to obtain a four-year degree, you can simply take courses from other departments. If you're attending a business school that doesn't offer classes beyond those needed directly for your job, you can take courses on your own at another school to create your own program. Whether you go for a certificate, diploma, or degree in your secretarial training, you may want to branch out into subjects completely different from your secretarial courses. These can give you a leg up in the job market and make your secretarial career more rewarding and creative.

Studying a second language, for example, can lead to jobs in other countries or in international organizations in this country. Studying fashion or film can give you an edge in these exciting fields. Casco Bay College, for instance, offers a seven-course certificate in travel and tourism or fashion merchandising designed for students who have obtained an associate of arts degree. Within its associate degree category, the ESS College for Business offers a bilingual option, in which you will use computer software in both English and Spanish, which will prepare you for a job in an international setting. Many other schools offer such programs or fit electives into the training program itself.

The Bachelor of Arts or Bachelor of Science Degree

There are no four-year programs offered strictly for administrative assistants. If you are interested in a bachelor's degree, the possibilities include majoring in business, which will give you a greater chance for advancement from an administrative assistant position to a higher position in a company or organization, perhaps even to a managerial position. Many administrative assistants work on a two-year degree in their field, and then spend the remaining two years taking business, financial, or other relevant courses (see the previous section on specialties). It's also possible to secure work as an administrative assistant with a liberal arts background. A diversified field of study that includes courses in literature, religion, philosophy, science, mathematics, and economics will prepare you for many future positions.

If you're worried about the time commitment, check around with the schools you're interested in. Many offer part-time study options, and night and weekend classes so that your education doesn't get in the way of your family or work obligations. If the cost of a four-year degree seems prohibitive, read Chapter 3, which covers the types of financial aid available to students in all fields.

Temporary Agency Courses

Temporary agencies routinely offer courses in office skills to their employees and staff members. Both Manpower and Kelly Services, for example, offer free software courses in a wide variety of applications. If you apply for temporary work at Kelly Services, you will be seated at one of the agency's computers, using their PinPoint® program. Developed by Kelly Services, PinPoint® tests for technological literacy at four levels. They begin with basic computer literacy, and then move to knowledge of applications such as Windows, word processing, spreadsheets, presentation graphics, databases, e-mail, and the Internet. The two highest levels cover topics such as DOS-based applications and desktop publishing. Once you've been tested, you will receive training in the areas needed. All computer training at Kelly Services is free.

Manpower offers a Global Learning Network, designed to teach a variety of business skills, such as new technologies and human resources management. Courses are offered online, so they may be accessed at any time. They generally take five hours to complete, and utilize hands-on exercises and testing. Manpower also provides a virtual Community Center, which connects you with others through live seminars and chat rooms. All the courses are free.

On-the-Job Training

If, after careful consideration, you decide you want to start work without special training, you may be able to learn the skills you need on the job. To bypass formal education, you will need to be certain of the kind of work you want to do, and secure a job in that field with an employer who is willing to train you. One advantage, obviously, is expense; you will receive a salary while training, rather than being unemployed and having the expense of training. Be aware that it is advisable—and probably necessary—to get some kind of formal training because, as discussed earlier, the nature of secretarial work is changing all the time and you will need to keep abreast of changes in technology.

Distance Education

Distance education—formerly referred to as correspondence school—is also an option for training. These programs differ from those offered at schools in that your instruction is given through a variety of delivery systems, rather than the traditional teacher-and-students-in-the-classroom setup. Some rely heavily on the computer, providing Web-based interactive lessons over the Internet, while others allow you to read texts and take exams at your own pace. Increasingly, interactive video broadcasts to distant sites are being used. This involves your attendance in one location to watch an instructor giving a lesson from another. You have the opportunity to interact with your teacher and other students through the use of video cameras and monitors.

The most attractive feature of distance learning is flexibility; for most of these programs, you can work in your home, at your own pace. You need to be highly organized, disciplined, and motivated to succeed in distance education, and some people shy away from it for these same reasons. If home study seems like the best option for you, use the same criteria that follows when choosing a program. Then also consider the type of delivery system used and determine not only your own familiarity with the technology (if any), but also whether the institution provides student training and technical assistance during the course. Find out how much interaction takes place among teachers and students during courses—are teachers available via phone, e-mail, or meeting in-person?

Ask the school for the names of former students whom you can contact for information about their experiences with the school. Get complete information on the course of study, and compare it with the curricula of schools you know to be reputable. Make sure that the distance education school you choose is accredited by an organization such as the Distance Education and Training Council (www.detc.org). The U.S. Department of Education can tell you about other accrediting agencies; contact them at 400 Maryland Avenue, SW, Washington, DC 20202-0498 (1-800-872-5327), or online at www.ed.gov. Finally, check with the Chamber of Commerce, the Better Business Bureau, or the attorney general's office in the state where the school is headquartered to see if the school has had complaints lodged against it.

The University of Northwestern Ohio's Administrative Assistant Associate degree is offered through CyberU in a distance format. Tuition for the 108-credit course of study is $18,360.00.

The curriculum is as follows:

Required Courses (20 required)
Administrative Block I/7
Administrative Block II/7
Contract Law/5
Introduction to Business/3
Written Communications/3
Introduction to Microcomputing/3
Developing Business Presentations/3
Spreadsheet Applications/3
Principles of Management/5
Business Math/5
Notehand Theory/5
Notehand Dictation/3
Records Management/3
Machine Transcription/2
Notehand Transcription/3
Keyboarding I/5
Keyboarding II/5
Word Processing Lab/2
Word Processing I/3

Advanced Machine Transcription/3

Advanced Document Formatting/3

Required Courses (8 required)

Success Strategies/1

Macroeconomics/3

Psychology/3

Introduction to Human Communication/3

Composition I/5

Advanced Composition/5

The American Political Scene/3

Portfolio Capstone/1

Elective Courses (1 course)

Advanced Psychology/3

Source: University of Northwestern Ohio, www.unoh.edu.

Sample Program Costs

NAME & LOCATION OF SCHOOL	PROGRAM	LENGTH OF PROGRAM	AWARD	TUITION (2001)
American Institute of Health Technology (Boise, Idaho)	Medical Secretary	30 weeks	C/D	$7,595
Davenport College (Granger, IN)	Accounting Assistant	24 months	A	$14,310
	Executive Assistant	24 months	A	$14,310
	Administrative Office Technology	24 months	A	$10,017
Metro Business College (Jefferson City, Missouri)	Administrative Assistant	33 weeks	C/D	$7,785
	Medical Administrative Assistant	38 weeks	C/D	$7,725
	Medical Secretary	44 weeks	C/D	$9,300
MTI Business College (Stockton, California)	Executive Secretary	36 weeks	C/D	$5,505
	Legal Secretary	36 weeks	C/D	$5,755
	Medical Secretary	37 weeks	C/D	$5,755
New York State Community Colleges	Administrative Assistant	24 months	A	$4,680 resident/ $9,360 non-resident
	Business Administration	24 months	A	

A= Associate's degree

C/D= certificate/diploma

CHOOSING A TRAINING PROGRAM

Selecting the training program that will best suit your needs, likes, and goals means making many decisions, including those about the type of school (community college, proprietary school, two- or four-year institution, or temp agency), overall size of the school, location, and quality of programs. Would you prefer a single-sex or co-ed environment? Large classes held in lecture halls or smaller classes in which you get to know your teachers? Do you want to go a local school and live at home, or are you willing to relocate and perhaps live in on-campus housing?

You can explore these options and many others by enlisting the help of an experienced high-school guidance counselor or career counselor. Keep asking questions—of yourself and them—until you have the information you need to make your decision. If you are not currently in school, use the guidebooks listed in this chapter, and the resources listed in the appendix at the end of this book, to help you. And whether in school or not, you should talk with those who are already working in your chosen field about their experiences. Ask where they went to school, what advantages they gained from their education, and what they would do differently if they were starting again.

Which Educational Setting is Right for You?

As mentioned earlier in this chapter, there are seven types of programs offered in a variety of settings. From your reading thus far, you probably have a good idea as to the program you're interested in, based on your current level of education and career goals. Read on to explore the types of schools and businesses that offer administrative assistant programs.

If you are interested in a certificate program, will live at home, and work while getting your education, you might consider a community college or proprietary school. Community colleges are public institutions offering vocational and academic courses both during the day and at night. They typically cost less than both two- and four-year public and private institutions. Proprietary schools are privately owned, but also tend to cost less than two-

and four-year schools. Both community colleges and proprietary institutions usually require a high school diploma or GED for admission.

You can find out the location of community colleges in your area by contacting your state's Department of Higher Education (listed in Appendix A). Or check the Web through a search engine, such as Yahoo.com, for community colleges, which are listed by state. Proprietary schools may also be found on the Internet. Use the search terms "administrative assistant education" to get started.

Junior colleges are two-year institutions that are usually more expensive than community colleges because they tend to be privately owned. You can earn a two-year degree (Associate of Arts or Associate of Science), which can usually be applied to four-year programs at most colleges and universities. Use the Internet or *Peterson's Two-Year Colleges* to help you with your search.

Colleges and universities offer undergraduate (usually four-year) programs in which you can earn a bachelor's degree in a variety of fields. Entrance requirements are more stringent than for community colleges; admissions personnel will expect you to have taken certain classes in high school to meet their admission standards. Your high school GPA (grade point average) and standardized test scores (most often the Scholastic Aptitude Test [SAT]) will be considered. If your high school grades are weak or it has been some time since you were last in school, you might want to consider taking courses at a community college first. You can always apply to the college or university as a transfer student after your academic track record has improved.

Be aware that state or public colleges and universities are less expensive to attend than private colleges and universities because they receive state funds to offset their operational costs. Another thing to consider when choosing a college is whether they have placement programs for administrative assistants. Do they have a relationship with those in the area who hire, in which the employers actively recruit on campus? Attending a school with such a relationship could greatly improve your chances of employment upon graduation.

Online College Guides

Most of these sites offer similar information, including various search methods, the ability to apply to many schools online, financial aid and scholarship information, and online test taking (PSAT, SAT, etc.). Some offer advice in selecting schools, give virtual campus tours, and help you decide what classes to take in high school. It is well worth it to visit several of them.

www.theadmissionsoffice.com—answers your questions about the application process, how to improve your chances of getting accepted, when to take tests

www.collegenet.com—on the Web since 1995, best for applying to schools online

www.collegequest.com—run by Peterson's, a well-known publisher of college guide books (they can also be found at www.petersons.com)

www.collegereview.com—offers good general information, plus virtual campus tours

www.embark.com—a good general site

www.review.com—a service of The Princeton Review. Plenty of insider information on schools, custom searches for school, pointers on improving standardized test scores

Evaluating Your Needs

We've discussed the types of training available, and the schools and businesses that offer them. Before making a final decision, you will want to consider two more things: your needs and the quality of the schools you are interested in. First, make a determination about what you want and need from a training program in terms of:

▶ location
▶ finances
▶ scheduling

Read through the descriptions of these concerns below, and make notes regarding your position on each of them.

Where to Get Your Training

There are excellent training programs offered at schools throughout the country. To select one, you will need to decide where you want to be while getting your education. As mentioned earlier, it makes sense to attend a program located in the geographical area in which you want to work, for a number of reasons. Markets vary even within states, so it's important that you know as much as you can about the area in which you will be working.

In addition, attending school where you will later work allows you to make contacts for future job hunting. Your school may help with job placement locally, and it may employ as teachers people who are in a position to hire administrative assistants. Your instructors can thus be later sources of employment. Networking is discussed in greater detail in Chapter 4, but keep in mind that having friends from school when you're out in the job market can be a big help.

Finances

Costs of the various programs, and the differences in costs between each type of school, have been touched on earlier. Now, you will need to think more specifically about what you can afford. While there are many sources of funding for your education (check out Chapter 3), and schools do sometimes offer full or partial scholarships, you will still need to spend some money in order to get a quality education. When evaluating the schools you're interested in, be sure to find out all the costs, not just tuition. You will have to purchase books, which can cost hundreds of dollars over the course of the program (and over a thousand dollars if you're considering a bachelor's degree). If you won't live at home, you will need to pay for room and board, which can total as much as your tuition at some schools. Will you need childcare while attending classes or have to drive long distances to get to school? Consider those additional costs when calculating how much you will have to spend.

Don't rule out any schools in which you have an interest at this point. Just be sure to gather as much information as you can about real cost of attendance. Read through Chapter 3 to understand all of your options regarding financing your education. Then, you will be prepared to make an informed decision about which program to attend in terms of what you can afford.

Scheduling

When making a choice about training, you should also think about your schedule and the commitments you may already have made. For instance, do you currently have a job you'd like to continue working at while you're in school? You will need to find a program that offers classes at times when you're not working. Will an internship interfere with your employment? It might be a good idea to speak with your employer about your plans and goals. He or she may be willing to offer some flexibility.

If you have young children at home or some other responsibility that requires your time, consider how you will manage both that responsibility and your education. Some schools offer low-cost childcare to their students. Or perhaps another family member or friend could help while you're attending classes or studying. Be sure to think through all of the potential obstacles to your training, and seek out ways to overcome them. The schools themselves may be a source of assistance as well, so don't hesitate to ask how other students have managed or how the school can accommodate you.

Another option is part-time attendance. If you are under financial constraints, you can spread the cost of the program over a greater amount of time. If you have young children at home, need to continue working while getting your education, or have another time constraint, part-time attendance can allow you the flexibility your busy schedule demands. But be aware that while both the financial and time commitments to the program are significantly reduced, it is only for the short term. In total, you will have spent the same, or more, time and money getting your degree or certificate.

When you've considered what you want in terms of type of program, location, costs, and scheduling, you will be able to make a decision about the type of school to attend. Now, you will need to evaluate those schools that meet your criteria in order to find the one that best suits your needs.

Evaluating the Schools

By now, you should be able to make decisions about the type of program and school you'd like to attend, significantly narrowing down the number of schools that you are considering. After consulting the resources in this chapter, make a list of the schools offering what you want. Then, for each entry on your list, ask the following questions. If you don't have enough information, call the school's admission director and either ask the questions directly, or request more information in the form of school brochures, course descriptions, and other documents. Since many schools have their own websites, you may be able to find your answers on the Internet.

What are the qualifications of the faculty?

There should be some faculty members with advanced degrees (M.A., M.B.A., Ph.D., J.D., etc.), and some with experience in the working world. The faculty should be accessible to students for conferences. Student Jennifer Bergin says she chose Casco Bay College in large part because of the college's excellent faculty, who have advanced degrees and a great deal of work experience.

What is the student–teacher ratio?

It's important that the student–teacher ratio not be too high. Education suffers if classrooms are too crowded or if a teacher has too many students to hope to see everyone who wishes to be seen for a private conference. According to one of the top national accrediting agencies, the Accrediting Council for Independent Colleges and Schools, a reasonable student–teacher ratio for skills training is 30 students to one teacher in a lecture setting and fifteen students to one teacher in a laboratory or clinical instruction setting. At very good schools the ratio is even better than the ACICS recommends. For instance, the prestigious Taylor Business Institution has a ratio of ten students to one teacher.

Does the school offer extensive computer training and the latest technology?

It's a good idea when you are visiting schools—and you should definitely visit the schools you're seriously considering—to ask to see their lab facilities. The most recent and best computer technology and training should be available to students; the labs should include the technology necessary for:

▶ courses in the latest software
▶ a good introductory course in microcomputer concepts and applications
▶ courses in advanced computer applications for business
▶ a course in desktop publishing
▶ courses in data entry, spreadsheets, graphics, and drawing

Part of the accreditation process of a school (discussed next) includes an evaluation of its technological facilities, as well as of its library and other instructional resources.

Is the school accredited?

It's important that the school you choose be accredited. Accreditation is a tough, complex process and ensures sound educational and ethical business practices at the schools involved. It's a process schools undergo voluntarily. Among other things, to be accredited as a business school the institution must:

▶ offer a postsecondary (that is, beyond high school), business-related education that leads to a postsecondary credential (such as a certificate, diploma, or degree)

▶ be licensed by the appropriate state education agency

▶ offer educational programs that help students develop skills to enhance their careers

▶ have a sufficient number of graduates to allow the accrediting agency to review the results of the institution's program

Some accrediting agencies are national, some regional. The name of the accrediting agency for the school you're interested in will probably be plainly printed on the school's general catalog, or you can obtain the name of the agency by calling the school. In addition, each accrediting agency will send you, free of charge, a directory of the schools it accredits.

If you would like a directory, or have a question about the school you've chosen, you may call the agency that accredits that school, and its personnel will help you. See Accrediting Agencies in Appendix A for names, addresses, and phone numbers of reputable accrediting agencies for secretarial or administrative schools. Remember if you choose a school that is not accredited, you cannot get financial aid through any government programs.

What is the school's job placement rate for graduates?

A school's job placement rate for graduates is extremely important. Usually schools offer placement services free of charge, often for the working lifetime of their graduates. All accredited private schools must place a percentage (determined to be reasonable by the accrediting agency) of their students in order to maintain accreditation. Many good schools boast placement rates of 90% or more.

A good job placement office will offer:

- ▶ resume writing and cover letter writing assistance
- ▶ job leads—full-time, part-time, permanent, and temporary
- ▶ networking opportunities with employers in the area (often begun as a part of an internship while the student is still in school)
- ▶ seminars on job-hunting
- ▶ career counseling and simulated interviews
- ▶ lifetime placement assistance for graduates

Does the school have a good internship program?

The value of internships is discussed later, but you should look for a good internship program when deciding on an administrative assistant training program. The variety of internships makes schools located near a large city especially attractive. As part of the accreditation process, schools must monitor the internship programs to ensure the student is introduced to meaningful work, not simply relegated to filing or other menial tasks. A good internship will give you many advantages when you're ready to find your first job.

ADMISSION REQUIREMENTS

Basic admission requirements are similar for all good schools. To get an idea of the requirements you will have to meet for your training, look at those from the Katharine Gibbs School. They have been in operation for over 85 years, have nine locations in the northeastern United States, and offer an Executive Office Professional certificate program. In order to be accepted at Katharine Gibbs, you must have a high school diploma or GED, as well as an acceptable score on the CPAt (140 or higher—the CPAt test is administered at the Katharine Gibbs School). The applicant must then:

▶ complete a formal application and submit it to the admissions office, along with a nonrefundable $50 application fee

▶ interview with an admissions representative, a process that takes approximately one hour

▶ be recommended to the school president by the admissions representative

▶ complete an enrollment agreement

▶ request and submit an official high school transcript

▶ provide proof of required immunizations for certain schools

After you've completed the process, the school president will evaluate your application. Acceptances before high school graduation depend upon notification of satisfactory completion of high school requirements. Applicants who have concluded their junior year of high school may apply for early acceptance. As is the case with all schools accredited by a reputable accrediting agency, Katherine Gibbs has an excellent placement service to help you move from student to employee.

MAKING THE MOST OF YOUR TRAINING

Once you've chosen a program of study, completed the application process, and have then been accepted, there are a number of ways to guarantee that the time, effort, and money you spend on the program are maximized.

Internships

An internship is one way to get job experience before you enter the real workforce. Many training programs include internships as part of their curriculum. Although there are basically three types, all internships are designed as learning experiences, giving the intern exposure to an actual working environment. Internships can be one of the following:

▶ paid—the intern receives a salary for his/her work

▶ college—the intern is a student, and usually receives college credit for his/her work

▶ summer—the intern is likely to be a student, who may or may not receive college credit

Opportunities for administrative assistant internships may be found in law offices, medical offices, government agencies, banks, or other businesses or corporations. College internships may be the easiest to find because your school will place you, or help place you, in one. They have relationships with the offices and agencies that use interns, and place students with these companies year after year. The companies that offer internships may also look to hire students when they complete their courses of study. For a college internship, you may also have to attend a class with other interns, prepare a journal detailing your work experience, or write a paper about it.

If your school does not provide help in finding internships or does not offer credit for them, you can find one for yourself. There are a number of ways in which you can uncover an opportunity, either during the summer, a semester off, or once you have graduated. If your school hires lawyers to teach some courses, consider enrolling in them. You may be able to make a contact or contacts that could lead to an internship. The Internet is also a good source of information. There, you can learn about all stages of the internship experience, including identifying learning objectives, finding the right office, managing office politics, self-monitoring and documentation, and how to use the internship to land a permanent job. Three sites that offer listings of internships available nationwide are www.internships.com, www.internjobs.com, and www.vault.com.

The following books are also excellent resources:

Anselm, John. *The Yale Daily News Guide to Internships 2000* (New York: Kaplan, 2000).

Ehrlich Green, Marianne. *Internship Success* (New York: McGraw Hill, 1998).

Peterson's Internships 2001: The Largest Source of Internships Available (Princeton, NJ: Peterson's Guides, 2001).

When you locate specific internship opportunities, some of the questions you will want to ask include:

▶ How many work hours are required to receive credit?

▶ If applicable, how much does the internship pay?

▶ Will you be graded for your work? If so, by a college professor or the person you work under at the company you intern for?

▶ Do you have to arrange your own internship with the company or work through your school?

▶ Does the internship program at your school also require you to attend classes, write a paper, or make a presentation to a faculty member in order to receive credit?

▶ What will your responsibilities be on a day-to-day basis?

▶ Who, within the company, will you be working for?

▶ Will the internship provide real world work experience that's directly related to your chosen field?

▶ Will your participation in the internship provide you with networking opportunities?

Once you land an internship, consider it an audition for ultimately obtaining a full-time job. Always act professionally, ask questions, follow directions, display plenty of enthusiasm, volunteer to take on additional responsibilities, meet deadlines, and work closely with your boss/supervisor. Upon graduating, make sure to highlight your internship work on your resume. Having an internship on your resume will make you stand out to a recruiter for a number of reasons:

▶ you are already familiar with a professional environment and know what is expected of you

▶ you have proven yourself through performance to a potential employer

▶ after evaluating the realities of the job, you are still eager to pursue it

For all of the reasons detailed above, it makes great sense for you to get an internship. Claire Andrews, director of paralegal programs at Casco Bay College in Portland, Maine notes, "It's really important to me that the students do get out there, whether it's through a part-time job or through the internship, to get the practical experience. Otherwise, waving that certificate means nothing."

Getting the Most Out of Your Classes

Here are three things you must do in order to get the most out of your classes:

▶ complete all assignments before class
▶ take good notes both while completing assignments, and during class; an outline style of note-taking works best to organize information and make studying easier
▶ ask questions about anything you don't understand as topics are introduced; do not wait until exam time

Preparing for Exams

Begin preparing for an exam by reading over your notes. Look for any areas that you indicated you didn't understand at the time, and make sure you understand them now. If you don't, talk to your instructor or do some extra reading until the concept is clear. Then try making an outline of the class. If you've taken good notes all along, you will simply put each day's notes in order. But if your notes are less than perfect, create an outline to study from.

Most important, on the evening before the exam, relax, eat a good dinner, and get a good night's sleep. In the morning, eat a good breakfast (and lunch, if it's an afternoon test). Try to take a walk or get some other light exercise, if you have time before the exam. During the exam, stay calm and have faith in yourself and your abilities.

Your Social Life

During your training program, there will be interesting people sitting next to you in class and teaching your classes. These people have experiences and knowledge that can be a benefit to you. You can help each other by studying together and creating an information loop that keeps everyone informed not only about what is happening in class, but throughout the school as well.

Forging friendships with teachers and students can make the transition from student to administrative assistant easier as well. After graduation, these are the people who may be able to help you get your first job. They may also be your colleagues throughout your career.

If the program you're in offers social events, take advantage of them as often as you can. And make it a point early in your academic career to get to know those in your counseling and placement offices. These people know the answers to almost all your questions, and can be an invaluable resource.

Your administrative assistant training is the first step on the road to your chosen career. Don't view it simply as something to get through, as an ordeal you must overcome before you can begin work and start your real life. School is the time to learn as much about the profession and yourself as you possibly can. Along the way, you will make friends and contacts—sometimes they will be the same person—who will be equally valuable to you as you finish school and embark on your career.

THE INSIDE TRACK

Who: Siobhán Flahive

What: Editorial Assistant

Where: LearningExpress

INSIDER'S STORY

After college, I was interested in getting into publishing, but I didn't really have enough experience to start in an editorial position. I have a bachelor's degree in writing, and also some background in education. I took a job as an administrative assistant with a scientific publishing company. My duties there were unrelated to the editing side of the business, but the work did give me a better idea of how a publishing company operates. More importantly, it gave me an edge when I did decide to switch jobs; having experience in publishing made it much easier to get a job with another publishing company.

In my current job, I work with a small group of editors. Some of the work I do is editorial (like proofreading), but a lot of my duties are administrative. I send out contracts to authors, answer the phones, do some data entry for our online tests, and draft corre-spondence. In my previous job, I was more of a general office assistant.

Some people don't really understand the level of organization that it takes to do administrative work well. Most of my coworkers have been very appreciative, but once in a while you encounter someone who talks down to you or wants you to do work that's outside the scope of your job. The best way to handle a difficult situation is to keep it from escalating. One of the most useful things I learned in my previous job was staying calm under pressure, and not making things worse by getting angry or irritated. It's essential to be able to interact with all kinds of people in a professional way.

While I never pursued an administrative career per se, I've found that entry-level jobs in most fields will involve some degree of administrative work. Computer skills are absolutely necessary; every job I looked at required some degree of familiarity with applications like Word and Excel. Besides computer skills, it's important to be able to handle several projects at once, and know how to prioritize so that you use your time effectively. Even if you decide not to remain in the administrative field, these kinds of skills will be valuable in almost any job.

CHAPTER three

FINANCING YOUR EDUCATION

Postsecondary education of any kind and duration can be quite expensive. However, that's no reason not to go to school; if you are determined to get training, there's financial aid available for you. This chapter explains the three types of financial aid available: scholarships and grants, loans, and work-study programs. You will find out how to determine your eligibility, which financial records you will need to gather, and how to complete and file forms (a sample financial aid form is included). At the end of the chapter, many resources are listed that can help you find the aid you need.

YOU HAVE decided on a career as an administrative assistant, and you've chosen a training program. Now, you need a plan for financing your training. Perhaps you or your family has been saving for your education, and you've got the money to pay your way. However, if you're like most students, you don't have enough to cover the cost of the training program you'd like to attend. Be assured that you can usually qualify for financial aid, even if you plan to attend school only part-time.

Because there are many types of financial aid, and the millions of dollars given away or loaned are available through so many sources, the process of finding funding for your education can seem confusing. Read through this chapter carefully and check out the many resources, including websites and publications, listed in Appendix B. You will have a better understanding of where to look for financial aid, what you can qualify for, and how and when to apply.

Also take advantage of the financial aid office of the school you've chosen, or your guidance counselor if you're still in high school. These professionals can also offer plenty of information and can help to guide you through the process. If you're not in school and haven't chosen a program yet, look to the Internet. It's probably the best source for up-to-the-minute information, and almost all of it is free. There are a number of great sites at which you can fill out questionnaires with information about yourself, and receive lists of scholarships and other forms of financial aid for which you may qualify. You can also apply for some types of federal and state aid online.

SOME MYTHS ABOUT FINANCIAL AID

The subject of financial aid is often misunderstood. Here are three of the most common myths:

Myth #1. All the red tape involved in finding sources and applying for financial aid is too confusing for me.

Fact: It's really not that confusing. The whole financial aid process is a set of steps that are ordered and logical. Besides, several sources of help are available. To start, read this chapter carefully to get a helpful overview of the entire process and tips on how to get the most financial aid. Then, use one or more of the resources listed within this chapter and in the appendices for additional help. If you believe you will be able to cope with college, you will be able to cope with looking for the money to finance your education, especially if you take the process one step at a time in an organized manner.

Myth #2: For most students, financial aid just means getting a loan and going into heavy debt, which isn't worth it, or working while in school, which will lead to burnout and poor grades.

Fact: Both the federal government and individual schools award grants and scholarships, which the student doesn't have to pay back. It is also possible to get a combination of scholarships and loans. It's worth taking out a loan if it means attending the school you really want to attend, rather than settling for your second choice or not going to school at all. As for working while in school, it's true that it is a challenge to hold down a full-time or even part-time job while in school. However, a small amount of work-study employment (10–12 hours per week) has been shown to actually improve academic performance because it teaches students important time-management skills.

Myth #3. I can't understand the financial aid process because of all the unfamiliar terms and strange acronyms that are used.

Fact: While you will encounter an amazing number of acronyms and some unfamiliar terms while applying for federal financial aid, you can refer to the acronym list and glossary at the end of this chapter for quick definitions and clear explanations of the commonly used terms and acronyms.

TYPES OF FINANCIAL AID

There are three categories of financial aid:

1. Grants and scholarships—aid that you don't have to pay back
2. Work-Study—aid that you earn by working
3. Loans—aid that you have to pay back

Each of these types of financial aid will be examined in greater detail, so you will be able to determine which one(s) to apply for, and when and how to apply. Note that the first two types of aid are available on four levels: federal, state, school, and private.

Grants

Grants are normally awarded based on financial need. Even if you believe you won't be eligible based on your own or your family's income, don't skip this section. There are some grants awarded for academic performance and other criteria. The two most common grants, the Pell Grant and Supplemental Educational Opportunity Grant (SEOG), are both offered by the federal government.

Federal Pell Grants

Federal Pell Grants are based on financial need and are awarded only to undergraduate students who have not yet earned a bachelor's or professional degree. For many students, Pell Grants provide a foundation of financial aid to which other aid may be added. For the year 1999–2000, the maximum award was $3,125.00. You can receive only one Pell Grant in an award year, and you may not receive Pell Grant funds for more than one school at a time.

How much you get will depends not only on your Expected Family Contribution (EFC) but also on your cost of attendance, whether you're a full-time or part-time student, and whether you attend school for a full academic year or less. It is possible to qualify for a Pell Grant even if you are only enrolled part-time in a training program. You should also be aware that some private and school-based sources of financial aid will not consider your eligibility if you haven't first applied for a Pell Grant.

Federal Supplemental Educational Opportunity Grants (FSEOG)

FSEOGs are for undergraduates with exceptional financial need—that is, students with the lowest Expected Family Contributions (EFCs). They give priority to students who receive Pell Grants. An FSEOG is similar to a Pell Grant in that it doesn't need to be paid back.

You can receive between $100 and $4,000 a year, depending on when you apply, your level of need, and the funding level of the school you're attending. There's no guarantee that every eligible student will be able to receive a FSEOG. Students at each school are paid based on the availability of funds at that school and not all schools participate in this program. To have the best chances of getting this grant, apply as early as you can after January 1 of the year in which you plan to attend school.

State Grants

State grants may be specific to the state in which you receive your education, in which you reside, or in which your parents reside. If you and your parents live in the state in which you will attend school, you've got only one place to check. However, if you will attend school in another state, or your parents live in another state, be sure to check them all; residency and eligibility requirements vary. There is a list of state agencies in Appendix A, including telephone numbers and websites, so you can easily find out if there is a grant for which you can apply.

Scholarships

Scholarships are often awarded for academic merit or for special characteristics (for example, ethnic heritage, personal interests, sports, parents' career, college major, geographic location) rather than financial need. As with grants, you do not pay your award money back. Scholarships may be offered from federal, state, school, and private sources.

The best way to find scholarship money is to use one of the free search tools available on the Internet. After entering the appropriate information about yourself, a search takes place which ends with a list of those prizes for which you are eligible. Try www.fastasp.org, which bills itself as the world's largest and oldest private sector scholarship database. www.college-scholarships.com and www.gripvision.com are also good sites for conducting searches. If you don't have easy access to the Internet, or want to expand your search, your high school guidance counselors or college financial aid officers also have plenty of information about available scholarship money. Also, check out your local library.

To find private sources of aid, spend a few hours in the library looking at scholarship and fellowship books or consider a reasonably priced (under $30) scholarship search service. See the Resources section at the end of this chapter to find contact information for search services and scholarship book titles. Also contact some or all of the professional associations for administrative assistants; some offer scholarships, while others offer information about where to find scholarships. If you're currently employed, find out if your employer has aid funds available. If you're a dependent student, ask your parents and other relatives to check with groups or organizations they belong to for possible aid sources. Consider these popular sources of scholarship money:

religious organizations
fraternal organizations
clubs, such as the Rotary, Kiwanis, American Legion, or 4-H
athletic clubs
veterans groups
ethnic group associations
unions

If you already know which school you will attend, check with a financial aid administrator (FAA) in the financial aid department to find out if you qualify for any school-based scholarships or other aid. Many schools offer merit-based aid for students with a high school GPA of a certain level or with a certain level of SAT scores in order to attract more students to their school. Check with the administrative assistant program's academic department to see if they maintain a bulletin board or other method of posting available scholarships.

While you are looking for sources of scholarships, continue to enhance your chances of winning one by participating in extracurricular events and volunteer activities. You should also obtain references from people who know you well and are leaders in the community, so you can submit their names and/or letters with your scholarship applications. Make a list of any awards you've received in the past or other honors that you could list on your scholarship application.

A program benefiting mainly middle-class students is the Hope Scholarship Credit. Eligible taxpayers may claim a credit for tuition and fees up to a maximum of $1,500.00 per student (the amount is scheduled to be re-indexed for inflation in 2002). The credit applies only to the first two years of postsecondary education, and students must be enrolled at least half-time. Families whose adjusted gross income is $80,000.00 or more are ineligible. To find out more about the Hope Scholarship credit, log onto www.sfas.com.

The National Merit Scholarship Corporation offers about 5,000 students scholarship money each year based solely on academic performance in high school. If you are a high school senior with excellent grades and high scores on tests such as the SAT, ask your guidance counselor for details about this scholarship.

You may also be eligible to receive a scholarship from your state (again, generally the state you reside in) or school. Check with the higher education department of the relevant state or states, or the financial aid office of the school you will attend.

Work-Study Programs

When applying to a college or university, you can indicate that you are interested in a work-study program. Their employment office will have the most information about how to earn money while getting your education. Work options include the following:

- ▶ on- or off-campus
- ▶ part-time or almost full-time
- ▶ school- or nationally based
- ▶ in the administrative field (to gain experience) or not (just to pay the bills)
- ▶ for money to repay student loans or to go directly toward educational expenses

If you're interested in school-based employment, you will be given the details about the types of jobs offered (they can range from giving tours of the campus to prospective students, to working in the cafeteria, or helping other students in the financial aid office) and how much they pay.

You may also want to investigate the Federal Work-Study (FWS) program, which can be applied for on the FAFSA. The FWS program provides jobs for undergraduate and graduate students with financial need, allowing them to earn money to help pay education expenses. It encourages community service work and provides hands-on experience related to your course of study, when available. The amount of the FWS award depends on:

▶ when you apply (apply early!)
▶ your level of need
▶ the funds available at your particular school

FWS salaries are the current federal minimum wage or higher, depending on the type of work and skills required. As an undergraduate, you will be paid by the hour (a graduate student may receive a salary), and you will receive the money directly from your school; you cannot be paid by commission or fee. The awards are not transferable from year to year, and you will need to check with the schools to which you're applying: not all schools have work-study programs in every area of study.

An advantage of working under the FWS program is that your earnings are exempt from FICA taxes if you are enrolled full-time and are working less than half-time. You will be assigned a job on-campus, in a private non-profit organization, or a public agency that offers a public service. You may provide a community service relating to fire or other emergency service if your school has such a program. Some schools have agreements with private for-profit companies, if the work demands your fire or other emergency skills. The total hourly wages you earn in each year cannot exceed your total FWS award for that year and you cannot work more than twenty hours per week. Your financial aid administrator (FAA) or the direct employer must consider your class schedule and your academic progress before assigning your job.

For more information about National Work Study programs, visit the Corporation for National Service website (www.cns.gov) and/or contact:

▶ National Civilian Community Corps (NCCC)—This AmeriCorps program is an 11-month residential national service program intended for 18–24 year olds. Participants receive $4,725.00 for college tuition or to help repay education loan debt. Contact:
National Civilian Community Corps
1100 Vermont Avenue NW
Washington, DC 20525
800-94-ACORPS

▶ Volunteers in Service to America (VISTA)—VISTA is a part of ACTION, the deferral domestic volunteer agency. This program offers numerous benefits to college graduates with outstanding student loans. Contact:

VISTA
1000 Wisconsin Ave. NW
Washington, DC 20007
800-424-8867

Student Loans

Although scholarships, grants, and work-study programs can help to offset the costs of higher education, they usually don't give you enough money to entirely pay your way. Most students who can't afford to pay for their entire education rely at least in part on student loans. The largest single source of these loans, and for all money for students, is the federal government. However, you can also find loan money from your state, school, and/or private sources.

Try these three sites for information about the United States government's programs:

www.fedmoney.org
This site explains everything from the application process (you can actually download the applications you will need), eligibility requirements, and the different types of loans available.

www.finaid.org
Here, you can find a calculator for figuring out how much money your education will cost (and how much you will need to borrow), get instructions for filling out the necessary forms, and even information on the various types of military aid (which will be detailed in the next chapter).

www.ed.gov/offices/OSFAP/students
The Federal Student Financial Aid Homepage. The FAFSA (Free Application for Federal Student Aid) can be filled out and submitted online. You can find a sample FAFSA in Appendix C, to help familiarize yourself with its format.

You can also get excellent detailed information about different sources of federal education funding by sending away for a copy of the U.S. Department of Education's publication, *The Student Guide*. Write to:

Federal Student Aid Information Center
P.O. Box 84
Washington, DC 20044
800-4FED-AID

The following are some of the most popular federal loan programs:

Federal Perkins Loans

A Perkins Loan has the lowest interest (currently, it's 5%) of any loan available for both undergraduate and graduate students, and is offered to students with exceptional financial need. You repay your school, which lends the money to you with government funds.

Depending on when you apply, your level of need, and the funding level of the school, you can borrow up to $4,000 for each year of undergraduate study. The total amount you can borrow as an undergraduate is $20,000.

The school pays you directly by check or credits your tuition account. You have nine months after you graduate (provided you were continuously enrolled at least half-time) to begin repayment, with up to ten years to pay off the entire loan.

PLUS Loans (Parent Loans for Undergraduate Students)

PLUS Loans enable parents with good credit histories to borrow money to pay education expenses of a child who is a dependent undergraduate student enrolled at least half-time. Your parents must submit the completed forms to your school.

To be eligible, your parents will be required to pass a credit check. If they don't pass, they might still be able to receive a loan if they can show that extenuating circumstances exist or if someone who is able to pass the credit check agrees to co-sign the loan. Your parents must also meet citizenship requirements.

The yearly limit on a PLUS Loan is equal to your cost of attendance minus any other financial aid you receive. For instance, if your cost of attendance is $6,000 and you receive $4,000 in other financial aid, your parents could borrow up to, but no more than, $2,000. The interest rate varies, but is not to exceed 9% over the life of the loan. Your parents must begin repayment while you're still in school. There is no grace period.

Federal Stafford Loans

Stafford Loans are low-interest loans that are given to students who attend school at least half-time. The maximum amount you can borrow is $23,000. The lender is the U.S. Department of Education if your school participates in their Direct Lending program or a bank or credit union if it does not. Stafford Loans fall into one of two categories:

- ▶ *Subsidized loans* are awarded on the basis of financial need. You will not be charged any interest before you begin repayment or during authorized periods of deferment. The federal government subsidizes the interest during these periods.
- ▶ *Unsubsidized loans* are not awarded on the basis of financial need. You will be charged interest from the time the loan is disbursed until it is paid in full. If you allow the interest to accumulate, it will be capitalized—that is, the interest will be added to the principal amount of your loan, and additional interest will be based upon the higher amount. This will increase the amount you have to repay.

There are many borrowing limit categories to these loans, depending on whether you get an unsubsidized or subsidized loan, which year in school you're enrolled, how long your program of study is, and if you're independent or dependent. You can have both kinds of Stafford Loans at the same time, but the total amount of money loaned at any given time cannot exceed $15,000. The interest rate varies, but cannot exceed 8.25%. An origination fee for a Stafford Loan is approximately 3% or 4% of the loan, and the fee will be deducted from each loan disbursement you receive. There is a six-month grace period after graduation before you must start repaying the loan.

State Loans

Loan money is also available from state governments. In Appendix A you will find a list of the agencies responsible for giving out such loans, with websites and other contact information. Remember that you may be able to qualify for a state loan based on your residency or your parents' residency.

Questions to Ask Before You Take out a Loan

In order to get the facts regarding the loan you're about to take out, ask the following questions:

1. What is the interest rate and how often is the interest capitalized? Your college's financial aid administrator (FAA) should be able to tell you this.

2. What fees will be charged? Government loans generally have an origination fee that goes to the federal government to help offset its costs, and a guarantee fee, which goes to a guaranty agency for insuring the loan. Both are deducted from the amount given to you.

3. Will I have to make any payments while still in school? Usually you won't and, depending on the type of loan, the government may even pay the interest for you while you're in school.

4. What is the grace period—the period after my schooling ends—during which no payment is required? Is the grace period long enough, realistically, for you to find a job and get on your feet? A six-month grace period is common.

5. When will my first payment be due and approximately how much will it be? You can get a good preview of the repayment process from the answer to this question.

6. Who exactly will hold my loan? To whom will I be sending payments? Who should I contact with questions or inform of changes in my situation? Your loan may be sold by the original lender to a secondary market institution, in which case you will be notified as to the contact information for your new lender.

7. Will I have the right to prepay the loan, without penalty, at any time? Some loan programs allow prepayment with no penalty but others do not.

8. Will deferments and forbearances be possible if I am temporarily unable to make payments? You need to find out how to apply for a deferment or forbearance if you need it.

9. Will the loan be canceled ("forgiven") if I become totally and permanently disabled, or if I die? This is always a good option to have on any loan you take out.

APPLYING FOR FINANCIAL AID

Now that you're aware of the types and sources of aid available, you will want to begin applying as soon as possible. You've heard about the Free Application for Federal Student Aid (FAFSA) many times in this chapter already, and have an idea of its importance. This is the form used by federal and state governments, as well as school and private funding sources, to determine your eligibility for grants, scholarships, and loans. The easiest way to get a copy is to log onto www.ed.gov/offices/OSFAP/students, where you can find help in completing the FAFSA and then submit the form electronically when you are finished. You can also get a copy by calling 1-800-4-FED-AID, or stopping by your public library or your school's financial aid office. Be sure to get an original form, because photocopies of federal forms are not accepted.

The second step of the process is to create a financial aid calendar. Using any standard calendar, write in all of the application deadlines for each step of the financial aid process. This way, all vital information will be in one location, so you can see at a glance what needs to be done when. Start this calendar by writing in the date you requested your FAFSA. Then mark down when you received it and when you sent in the completed form. Add important dates and deadlines for any other applications you need to complete for school-based or private aid as you progress though the financial aid process. Using and maintaining a calendar will help the whole financial aid process run more smoothly and give you peace of mind that the important dates are not forgotten.

When to Apply

Apply for financial aid as soon as possible after January 1 of the year in which you want to enroll in school. For example, if you want to begin school in the fall of 2002, then you should apply for financial aid as soon as possible after January 1, 2002. It is easier to complete the FAFSA after you have completed your tax return, so you may want to consider filing your taxes as early as possible as well. Do not sign, date, or send your application before January 1 of the year for which you are seeking aid. If you apply by mail, send your completed application in the envelope that came with the original application. The envelope is already addressed, and using it will make sure your application reaches the correct address.

Many students lose out on thousands of dollars in grants and loans because they file too late. A financial aid administrator from New Jersey says:

> When you fill out the Free Application for Federal Student Aid (FAFSA), you are applying for all aid available, both federal and state, work-study, student loans, etc. The important thing is complying with the deadline date. Those students who do are considered for the Pell Grant, the SEOG (Supplemental Educational Opportunity Grant) and the Perkins Loan, which is the best loan as far as interest goes. Lots of students miss the June 30th deadline, and it can mean losing $2,480 from TAG (Tuition Assistance Grant), about $350 from WPCNJ, and another $1,100 from EOF (Equal Opportunity Fund). Students, usually the ones who need the money most, often ignore the deadlines.

After you mail in your completed FAFSA, your application will be processed in approximately four weeks. Then you will receive a Student Aid Report (SAR) in the mail. The SAR will disclose your Expected Family Contribution (EFC), the number used to determine your eligibility for federal student aid. Each school you list on the application may also receive your application information if the school is set up to receive it electronically.

You must reapply for financial aid every year. However, after your first year, you will receive a Student Aid Report (SAR) in the mail before the application deadline. If no corrections need to be made, you can just sign it and send it in.

Getting Your Forms Filed

Follow these three simple steps if you are not completing and submitting the FAFSA online:

1. Get an original Federal Application for Federal Student Aid (FAFSA). Remember to pick up an original copy of this form, as photocopies are not acceptable.

2. Fill out the entire FAFSA as completely as possible. Make an appointment with a financial aid counselor if you need help. Read the forms completely, and don't skip any relevant portions.

3. Return the FAFSA before the deadline date. Financial aid counselors warn that many students don't file the forms before the deadline and lose out on available aid. Don't be one of those students!

Financial Need

Financial aid from many of the programs discussed in this chapter is awarded on the basis of need (the exceptions include unsubsidized Stafford, PLUS, and Consolidation loans, and some scholarships and grants). When you apply for federal student aid by completing the FAFSA, the information you report is used in a formula established by the U. S. Congress. The formula determines your Expected Family Contribution (EFC), an amount you and your family are expected to contribute toward your education. If your EFC is below a certain amount, you will be eligible for a Pell Grant, assuming you meet all other eligibility requirements.

There is no maximum EFC that defines eligibility for the other financial aid options. Instead, your EFC is used in an equation to determine your financial needs.

Cost of Attendance – EFC = Financial Need

A financial aid administrator calculates your cost of attendance and subtracts the amount you and your family are expected to contribute toward that cost. If there's anything left over, you're considered to have financial need.

Are You Considered Dependent or Independent?

Federal policy uses strict and specific criteria to make this designation, and that criteria applies to all applicants for federal student aid equally. A dependent student is expected to have parental contribution to school expenses, and an independent student is not. The parental contribution depends on the number of parents with earned income, their income and assets, the age of the older parent, the family size, and the number of family members enrolled in postsecondary education. Income is not just the adjusted gross income from a tax return, but also includes nontaxable income such as Social Security benefits and child support.

You're an independent student if at least one of the following applies to you:

- ▶ you were born before January 1, 1978
- ▶ you're married (even if you're separated)
- ▶ you have legal dependents other than a spouse who get more than half of their support from you and will continue to get that support during the award year
- ▶ you're an orphan or ward of the court (or were a ward of the court until age 18)
- ▶ you're a graduate or professional student
- ▶ you're a veteran of the U.S. Armed Forces—formerly engaged in active service in the U.S. Army, Navy, Air Force, Marines, Coast Guard, or as a cadet or midshipman at one of the service academies—released under a condition other than dishonorable. (ROTC students, members of the National Guard, and most reservists are not considered veterans, nor are cadets and midshipmen still enrolled in one of the military service academies.)

If you live with your parents and if they claimed you as a dependent on their last tax return then your need will be based on your parents' income. You do not qualify for independent status just because your parents have decided to not claim you as an exemption on their tax return (this used to be the case but is no longer) or do not want to provide financial support for your college education.

Students are classified as *dependent* or *independent* because federal student aid programs are based on the idea that students (and their parents or spouse, if applicable) have the primary responsibility for paying for their postsecondary education.

Gathering Financial Records

Your financial need for most grants and loans depends on your financial situation. Now that you've determined whether you are considered a dependent or independent student, you will know whose financial records you need to gather for this step of the process. If you are a dependent student, then you must gather not only your own financial records, but also those of your parents because you must report their income and assets as well as your own when you complete the FAFSA. If you are an independent student, then you need to gather only your own financial records (and those of your spouse if you're married). Gather your tax records from the year prior to the one in which you are applying. For example, if you apply for the fall of 2002, you will use your tax records from 2001.

To Help You Fill Out the FAFSA, Gather the Following Documents:

- U.S. income tax returns (IRS Form 1040, 1040A, or 1040EZ) for the year that just ended and W-2 and 1099 forms
- Records of untaxed income, such as Social Security benefits, AFDC or ADC, child support, welfare, pensions, military subsistence allowances, and veterans' benefits
- Current bank statements and mortgage information
- Medical and dental expenses for the past year that weren't covered by health insurance
- Business and/or farm records
- Records of investments such as stocks, bonds, and mutual funds, as well as bank Certificates of Deposit (CDs) and recent statements from money market accounts
- Social Security number(s)

Even if you do not complete your federal income tax return until March or April, you should not wait to file your FAFSA until your tax returns are filed with the IRS. Instead, use estimated income information and submit the FAFSA, as noted earlier, just as soon as possible after January 1. Be as accurate as possible, knowing that you can correct estimates later.

Maximizing Your Eligibility for Loans and Scholarships

Loans and scholarships are often awarded based on an individual's eligibility. Depending on the type of loan or scholarship you pursue, the eligibility requirements will be different. EStudentLoan.com (www.estudentloan.com/workshop.asp) offers the following tips and strategies for improving your eligibility when applying for loans and/or scholarships:

1. Save money in the parent's name, not the student's name.
2. Pay off consumer debt, such as credit card and auto loan balances.
3. Parents considering going back to school should do so at the same time as their children. The more family members in school simultaneously, the more aid may be available to each.
4. Spend student assets and income first, before other assets and income.
5. If you believe that your family's financial circumstances are unusual, make an appointment with the financial aid administrator at your school to review your case. Sometimes the school will be able to adjust your financial aid package to compensate.
6. Minimize capital gains
7. Do not withdraw money from your retirement fund to pay for school. If you must use this money, *borrow* from your retirement fund.
8. Minimize educational debt.
9. Ask grandparents to wait until the grandchild graduates before giving them money to help with their education.
10. Trust funds are generally ineffective at sheltering money from the need analysis process, and can backfire on you.
11. If you have a second home and you need a home equity loan, take the equity loan on the second home and pay off the mortgage on the primary home.

GENERAL GUIDELINES FOR LOANS

Before you commit yourself to any loans, be sure to keep in mind that they need to be repaid. Estimate realistically how much you will earn when you leave school, remembering that you will have other monthly obligations such as housing, food, and transportation expenses.

Once You're in School

Once you have your loan (or loans) and are attending classes, don't forget about the responsibility of your loan. Keep a file of information on your loan that includes copies of all your loan documents and related correspondence, along with a record of all your payments. Open and read all your mail about your education loan.

Remember also that you are obligated by law to notify both your Financial Aid Administrator (FAA) and the holder or servicer of your loan if there is a change in your:

- ▶ name
- ▶ address
- ▶ enrollment status (dropping to less than half-time means that you will have to begin payment six months later)
- ▶ anticipated graduation date

After You Leave School

After graduation, you must begin repaying your student loan immediately or after the grace period. For example, if you have a Stafford Loan you will be provided with a six-month grace period before your first payment is due; other types of loans have grace periods as well. If you haven't been out in the workforce before, with your loan repayment you will begin your credit history. If you make payments on time, you will build up a good credit rating, and credit will be easier for you to obtain for other things. Get off to a good start so you don't run the risk of going into default. If you default (or refuse to pay back your loan) any number of the following things could happen to you as a result:

▶ have trouble getting any kind of credit in the future
▶ no longer qualify for federal or state educational financial aid
▶ have holds placed on your college records
▶ have your wages garnished
▶ have future federal income tax refunds taken
▶ have your assets seized

To avoid the negative consequences of going into default in your loan, be sure to do the following:

▶ Open and read all mail you receive about your education loans immediately.
▶ Make scheduled payments on time; since interest is calculated daily, delays can be costly.
▶ Contact your servicer immediately if you can't make payments on time; he or she may be able to get you into a graduated or income-sensitive/income contingent repayment plan or work with you to arrange a deferment or forbearance.

There are a few circumstances under which you won't have to repay your loan. If you become permanently and totally disabled, you probably will not have to (providing the disability did not exist prior to your obtaining the aid). Likewise if you die, if your school closes permanently in the middle of the term, or if you are erroneously certified for aid by the financial aid office. However, if you're simply disappointed in your program of study or don't get the job you wanted after graduation, you are not relieved of your obligation.

Loan Repayment

When it comes time to repay your loan, you will make payments to your original lender, to a secondary market institution to which your lender has sold your loan, or to a loan servicing specialist acting as its agent to collect payments. At the beginning of the process, try to choose the lender who offers you the best benefits (for example, a lender who lets you pay electronically, offers lower interest rates to those who consistently pay on time, or who has a toll-free number to call 24 hours a day, seven days a week). Ask the financial aid administrator at your college to direct you to such lenders.

Be sure to check out your repayment options before borrowing. Lenders are required to offer repayment plans that will make it easier to pay back your loans. Your repayment options may include:

▶ *Standard repayment*: full principal and interest payments due each month throughout your loan term. You will pay the least amount of interest using the standard repayment plan, but your monthly payments may seem high when you're just out of school.

▶ *Graduated repayment*: interest-only or partial interest monthly payments due early in repayment; payment amounts increase thereafter. Some lenders offer interest-only or partial interest repayment options, which provide the lowest initial monthly payments available.

▶ *Income-based repayment*: monthly payments are based on a percentage of your monthly income.

▶ *Consolidation loan*: allows the borrower to consolidate several types of federal student loans with various repayment schedules into one loan. This loan is designed to help student or parent borrowers simplify their loan repayments. The interest rate on a consolidation loan may be lower than what you're currently paying on one or more of your loans. The phone number for loan consolidation at the William D. Ford Direct Loan Program is 1-800-557-7392. Financial administrators recommend that you do not consolidate a Perkins Loan with any other loans since the interest on a Perkins Loan is already the lowest available. Loan consolidation is not available from all lenders.

▶ *Prepayment*: paying more than is required on your loan each month or in a lump sum is allowed for all federally sponsored loans at any time during the life of the loan without penalty. Prepayment will reduce the total cost of your loan.

It's quite possible—in fact likely—that while you're still in school your FFELP loan will be sold to a secondary market institution such as Sallie Mae. You will be notified of the sale by letter, and you need not worry if this happens—your loan terms and conditions will remain exactly the same or they may even improve. Indeed, the sale may give you repayment options and benefits that you would not have had otherwise. Your payments after you finish school and your requests for information should be directed to the new loan holder.

If you receive any interest-bearing student loans, you will have to attend exit counseling after graduation, where the loan lenders will tell you the total amount of debt and work out a payment schedule with you to determine the amount and dates of repayment. Many loans do not become due until at least six to nine months after you graduate, giving you a grace period. For example, you do not have to begin paying on the Perkins Loan until nine months after you graduate. This grace period is to give you time to find a good job and start earning money. However, during this time, you may have to pay the interest on your loan.

If for some reason you remain unemployed when your payments become due, you may receive an unemployment deferment for a certain length of time. For many loans, you will have a maximum repayment period of ten years (excluding periods of deferment and forbearance).

THE MOST FREQUENTLY ASKED QUESTIONS ABOUT FINANCIAL AID

Here are answers to the most frequently asked questions about student financial aid:

1. *I probably don't qualify for aid—should I apply for it anyway?*
   Yes. Many students and families mistakenly think they don't qualify for aid and fail to apply. Remember that there are some sources of aid that are not based on need. The FAFSA form is free—there's no good reason for not applying.
2. *Do I need to be admitted at a particular university before I can apply for financial aid?*

No. You can apply for financial aid any time after January 1. However, to receive the funds, you must be admitted and enrolled in school.

3. *Do I have to reapply for financial aid every year?*

Yes, and if your financial circumstances change, you may get either more or less aid. After your first year you will receive a Renewal Application which contains preprinted information from the previous year's FAFSA. Renewal of your aid also depends on your making satisfactory progress toward a degree and achieving a minimum GPA.

4. *Are my parents responsible for my educational loans?*

No. You alone are responsible, unless they endorse or co-sign your loan. Parents are, however, responsible for the federal PLUS Loans. If your parents (or grandparents or uncle or distant cousins) want to help pay off your loan, you can have your billing statements sent to their address.

5. *If I take a leave of absence from school, do I have to start repaying my loans?*

Not immediately, but you will after the grace period. Generally, though, if you use your grace period up during your leave, you will have to begin repayment immediately after graduation, unless you apply for an extension of the grace period before it's used up.

6. *If I get assistance from another source, should I report it to the student financial aid office?*

Yes—and, unfortunately, your aid amount may be lowered accordingly. But you will get into trouble later on if you don't report it.

7. *Are federal work-study earnings taxable?*

Yes, you must pay federal and state income tax, although you may be exempt from FICA taxes if you are enrolled full-time and work less than 20 hours a week.

8. *My parents are separated or divorced. Which parent is responsible for filling out the FAFSA?*

If your parents are separated or divorced, the custodial parent is responsible for filling out the FAFSA. The custodial parent is the parent with whom you lived the most during the past 12 months. Note that this is not necessarily the same as the parent who has legal custody. The question of which parent must fill out the FAFSA becomes complicated in many situations, so you should take your particular circumstance to the student financial aid office for help.

Financial Aid Checklist

_____Explore your options as soon as possible once you've decided to begin a training program.

_____Find out what your school requires and what financial aid they offer.

_____Complete and mail the FAFSA as soon as possible after January 1.

_____Complete and mail other applications by the deadlines.

_____Gather loan application information and forms from your college financial aid office.

_____Forward the filled-out loan application to your school's financial aid office. Remember to sign the application!

_____Carefully read all letters and notices from the school, the federal student aid processor, the need analysis service, and private scholarship organizations. Note whether financial aid will be sent before or after you are notified about admission, and how exactly you will receive the money.

_____Return any requested documentation promptly to your financial aid office.

_____Report any changes in your financial resources or expenses to your financial aid office so they can adjust your award accordingly.

_____Reapply each year.

Financial Aid Acronyms Key

COA	Cost of Attendance
CWS	College Work-Study
EFC	Expected Family Contribution
EFT	Electronic Funds Transfer
ESAR	Electronic Student Aid Report
ETS	Educational Testing Service
FAA	Financial Aid Administrator
FAF	Financial Aid Form
FAFSA	Free Application for Federal Student Aid
FAO	Financial Aid Office/Officer
FDSLP	Federal Direct Student Loan Program
FFELP	Federal Family Education Loan Program
FSEOG	Federal Supplemental Educational Opportunity Grant
FWS	Federal Work-Study

PC	Parent Contribution
PLUS	Parent Loan for Undergraduate Students
SAP	Satisfactory Academic Progress
SC	Student Contribution
USED	U.S. Department of Education

FINANCIAL AID TERMS CLEARLY DEFINED

Accrued interest—Interest that accumulates on the unpaid principal balance of your loan.

Capitalization of interest—Addition of accrued interest to the principal balance of your loan that increases both your total debt and monthly payments.

Default (you won't need this one, right?)—Failure to repay your education loan.

Deferment—A period when a borrower, who meets certain criteria, may suspend loan payments.

Delinquency (you won't need this one, either!)—Failure to make payments when due.

Disbursement—Loan funds issued by the lender.

Forbearance—Temporary adjustment to repayment schedule for cases of financial hardship.

Grace period—Specified period of time after you graduate or leave school during which you need not make payments.

Holder—The institution that currently owns your loan.

In-school grace, and **deferment interest subsidy**—Interest the federal government pays for borrowers on some loans while the borrower is in school, during authorized deferments, and during grace periods.

Interest-only payment—A payment that covers only interest owed on the loan and none of the principal balance.

Interest—Cost you pay to borrow money.

Lender (Originator)—Puts up the money when you take out a loan. Most lenders are financial institutions, but some state agencies and schools make loans too.

Origination fee—Fee, deducted from the principal, which is paid to the federal government to offset its cost of the subsidy to borrowers under certain loan programs.

Principal—Amount you borrow, which may increase as a result of capitalization of interest, and the amount on which you pay interest.

Promissory note—Contract between you and the lender that includes all the terms and conditions under which you promise to repay your loan.

Secondary markets—Institutions that buy student loans from originating lenders, thus providing lenders with funds to make new loans.

Servicer—Organization that administers and collects your loan. May be either the holder of your loan or an agent acting on behalf of the holder.

Subsidized Stafford Loans—Loans based on financial need. The government pays the interest on a subsidized Stafford Loan for borrowers while they are in school and during specified deferment periods.

Unsubsidized Stafford Loans—Loans available to borrowers, regardless of family income. Unsubsidized Stafford Loan borrowers are responsible for the interest during in-school, deferment periods, and repayment.

FINANCIAL AID RESOURCES

In addition to the sources listed throughout this chapter, these are additional resources that may be used to obtain more information about financial aid.

Telephone Numbers

Federal Student Aid Information Center (U.S. Department of Education)

Hotline	800-4-FED-AID, 800-433-3243
TDD Number for Hearing-Impaired	800-730-8913
For suspicion of fraud or abuse of federal aid	800-MIS-USED (800-647-8733)
Selective Service	847-688-6888
Immigration and Naturalization Service (INS)	415-705-4205
Internal Revenue Service (IRS)	800-829-1040
Social Security Administration	800-772-1213

National Merit Scholarship Corporation	708-866-5100
Sallie Mae's College AnswerSM Service	800-222-7183
Career College Association	202-336-6828
ACT: American College Testing Program (about forms submitted to the need analysis servicer)	916-361-0656
College Scholarship Service (CSS)	609-771-7725; TDD 609-883-7051
Need Access/Need Analysis Service	800-282-1550
FAFSA on the WEB Processing/Software Problems	800-801-0576

Websites

www.ed.gov/prog_info/SFAStudentGuide

The Student Guide is a free informative brochure about financial aid and is available online at the Department of Education's Web address listed here.

www.ed.gov/prog_info/SFA/FAFSA

This site offers students help in completing the FAFSA.

www.ed.gov/offices/OPE/t4_codes.html

This site offers a list of Title IV school codes that you may need to complete the FAFSA.

www.ed.gov/offices/OPE/express.html

This site enables you to fill out and submit the FAFSA online. You will need to print out, sign, and send in the release and signature pages.

www.career.org

This is the website of the Career College Association (CCA). It offers a limited number of scholarships for attendance at private proprietary schools. You can also contact CCA at 750 First Street, NE, Suite 900, Washington, DC 20002-4242.

www.salliemae.com

Website for Sallie Mae that contains information about loan programs.

Software Programs

Cash for Class
Tel: 800-205-9581
Fax: 714-673-9039

Redheads Software, Inc.
3334 East Coast Highway #216
Corona del Mar, CA 92625
E-mail: cashclass@aol.com

C-LECT Financial Aid Module
Chronicle Guidance Publications
P.O. Box 1190
Moravia, NY 13118-1190
Tel: 800-622-7284 or 315-497-0330
Fax: 315-497-3359

Peterson's Award Search
Peterson's
P.O. Box 2123
Princeton, NJ 08543-2123
Tel: 800-338-3282 or 609-243-9111
E-mail: custsvc@petersons.com

Pinnacle Peak Solutions (Scholarships 101)
Pinnacle Peak Solutions
7735 East Windrose Drive
Scottsdale, AZ 85260
Tel: 800-762-7101 or 602-951-9377
Fax: 602-948-7603

TP Software—Student Financial Aid Search
Software
TP Software
P.O. Box 532
Bonita, CA 91908-0532
Tel: 800-791-7791 or 619-496-8673
E-mail: mail@tpsoftware.com

Books and Pamphlets

The Student Guide
Published by the U.S. Department of Education, this is the handbook about federal aid programs. To get a printed copy, call 1-800-4-FED-AID.

Looking for Student Aid
Published by the U.S. Department of Education, this is an overview of sources of information about financial aid. To get a printed copy, call 1-800-4-FED-AID.

How Can I Receive Financial Aid for College?
Published from the ACCESS ERIC Parent Brochures website. Order a printed copy by calling 800-LET-ERIC or write to ACCESS ERIC, Research Blvd-MS 5F, Rockville, MD 20850-3172. Available online at www.eric.ed.gov/archives/fin-aid.htm.

Cassidy, David J. *The Scholarship Book 2002: The Complete Guide to Private-Sector Scholarships, Fellowships, Grants, and Loans for the Undergraduate.* (Englewood Cliffs, NJ: Prentice Hall, 2001).

Chany, Kalman A. and Geoff Martz. *Student Advantage Guide to Paying for College 1997 Edition.* (New York: The Princeton Review, 1997).

College Costs & Financial Aid Handbook, 18th ed. (New York: The College Entrance Examination Board, 1998).

Cook, Melissa L. *College Student's Handbook to Financial Assistance and Planning* (Traverse City, MI: Moonbeam Publications, 1991).

Davis, Kristen. *Financing College: How to Use Savings, Financial Aid, Scholarships, and Loans to Afford the School of Your Choice* (Washington, DC: Random House, 1996).

Hern, Davis and Joyce Lain Kennedy. *College Financial Aid for Dummies* (Foster City, CA: IDG, 1999).

Peterson's Scholarships, Grants and Prizes 2002 (Princeton, NJ: Peterson's, 2001).

Ragins, Marianne. *Winning Scholarships for College: An Insider's Guide* (New York: Henry Holt, 1994).

Scholarships, Grants & Prizes: Guide to College Financial Aid from Private Sources. (Princeton, NJ: Peterson's, 1998).

Schwartz, John. *College Scholarships and Financial Aid* (New York: Simon & Schuster/Macmillan, 1995).

Schlacter, Gail and R. David Weber. *Scholarships 2000* (New York: Kaplan, 1999).

Other Related Financial Aid Books

Annual Register of Grant Support (Chicago, IL: Marquis, annual).

A's and B's of Academic Scholarships (Alexandria, VA: Octameron, annual).

Chronicle Student Aid Annual (Moravia, NY: Chronicle Guidance, annual).

College Blue Book. Scholarships, Fellowships, Grants and Loans (New York: Macmillan, annual).

College Financial Aid Annual (New York: Prentice Hall, annual).

Directory of Financial Aids for Minorities (San Carlos, CA: Reference Service Press, biennial).

Directory of Financial Aids for Women (San Carlos, CA: Reference Service Press, biennial).

Financial Aids for Higher Education (Dubuque, IA: Wm. C. Brown, biennial).

Financial Aid for the Disabled and their Families (San Carlos, CA: Reference Service Press, biennial).

Leider, Robert and Ann. *Don't Miss Out: the Ambitious Student's Guide to Financial Aid* (Alexandria, VA: Octameron, annual).

Paying Less for College (Princeton, NJ: Peterson's, annual).

See Appendix C for a sample FAFSA form.

THE INSIDE TRACK

Who: Laurie Lawrence
What: Freelance Administrative Assistant
Where: Viacom/CBS Legal

INSIDER'S STORY

I worked in an administrative position at ABC for nine years. On a typical day there, I would proofread several types of agreements and go over trademark and copyright information as well as music licenses. I drafted and finalized ABCNews.com writer agreements. I was responsible for arranging all meetings and travel arrangements for one Vice President and one senior attorney. I handled all office manager duties for our section. My job also included heavy phone activity and interaction with professionals of all levels within and outside the company.

I don't have any formal administrative training. I'm pursuing a career as an actor and singer, and I support myself doing administrative work during the day. The positive aspect of this work, whether freelance or permanent, is that an administrative job usually allows you to have a life and gives you enough freedom to pursue goals outside of work. For me, this type of job allows me to go on auditions, leave to rehearse, etc. You don't have to take the job home with you.

I've learned that having the right contacts sometimes mean more than actual skill and talent—not only in the administrative field, but in all business. To conduct job searches after being laid off, I signed up with several temporary agencies and used the Internet, as well as friends who were working. The best resources turned out to be my friends' recommendations—actually, the only work and interviews I got were as a result of those recommendations. Several of my out-of-work friends have said the exact same thing. Sending a resume cold often will yield nothing; however, sending a resume for the exact same job at the exact same company through a friend gets you seen.

I think the most useful skills, not only in an administrative position, but in any job, are to be able to present a positive appearance, both physically and socially. Being able to interact with all types of people is a must; the biggest challenge I've encountered has been learning to work with many different types of people in a professional manner. Having a good command of language (both verbal and written) is also important. Furthermore, it is essential to be able to multi-task and handle pressure with a sense of humor.

Also, if you decide on an administrative career, be sure that you know the kind of company and industry you in which you want to work. If you want to be casual and flexible and not have to dress up or be corporate, steer clear of those types of environments or you won't be happy.

CHAPTER four

FINDING YOUR FIRST JOB

In this chapter you will read about the job search process, explaining the many ways to locate a future employer once your administrative assistant training is completed (and even give you some tips on how you may find a job while still in school). You will learn how to conduct your job search through networking, research, reading industry publications, using classified ads, utilizing online resources, visiting job fairs, and contacting job hotlines. Knowing how to find the best employment opportunities is the first step in the job search process.

NOW THAT you've finished, or nearly finished, the education you need to become an administrative assistant, you're ready to find employment in your chosen field. Even in this time of downsizing, the job market for entry-level assistants is good, according to the U.S. Department of Labor. In their *Occupational Outlook Handbook, 2000–01*, the Bureau of Labor Statistics reports that there are over three million secretaries currently employed in the United States. While no changes are expected in that number through 2008, job opportunities are projected to be plentiful, as there is always a need to replace workers who leave this large profession. Industries that will be hiring the greatest number of new administrative assistants are those experiencing rapid growth, such as health and legal services, personnel supply, computer and data processing, and management and public relations.

The job search process can be time consuming and stressful. But by reading this chapter, you will give yourself an advantage. You will learn how to set goals and formulate career and job objectives. Then, take an organized approach to the whole procedure by setting deadlines and staying on top of the details. You will also learn how to find and utilize the best resources available to you, including the Internet, your school's career placement office, and networking contacts.

WHAT KIND OF JOB DO YOU REALLY WANT?

A good job means something different to everyone. In order to work at one that's right for you, you will first need to decide what you're looking for. This should be the first step in the job search process, formulating your job objective. Perhaps your goal is to someday be executive secretary to the CEO of a multinational organization. Or, you may be a parent or an artist, and you want a job that's satisfying but that doesn't consume your every waking moment. Or, you might want to begin as an administrative assistant in a certain field and then move on to an executive position.

Or, perhaps you're not sure. If that's the case, before you begin your job search, take the time to decide on long-term and short-term career goals. Picture yourself in a fulfilling job next week, next year, and five years from now. Are you thinking in terms of one job, or several, moving up the corporate ladder? While you're exploring your needs and wants, write them down. Use two or three columns, for short and long-term planning. Keep in mind that your goals should:

▶ describe in detail what you want to accomplish
▶ be measurable, formulated in terms that can clearly be evaluated (for instance, "by next year, I will be employed by a large law firm")
▶ be challenging, taking energy and discipline to accomplish your goals
▶ be realistic and attainable
▶ have a definite point of completion (long-term goals should be broken up into short-term goals with definite target completion dates)

► be flexible; sometimes great opportunities come along that take you in new directions, but still lead toward your long-term goals

TAKING A DEADLINE-ORIENTED APPROACH TO YOUR JOB SEARCH EFFORTS

As discussed, landing a job can be a difficult task. You have to find job opportunities, create a resume, write cover letters, schedule interviews, perform research on companies, participate in interviews, make follow up calls, and keep track of all the potential employers you meet or correspond with. One way to help take the stress out of this whole procedure is to adopt an organized, deadline-oriented approach for finding a job as an administrative assistant.

Begin by purchasing (if you don't already own one) a personal planner, such as a Day-Timer®, or a personal digital assistant (PDA) such as a Palm Pilot® (www.palm.com). Before actually starting your job search, make a list of everything you will have to accomplish in order to land a job. Break up the big tasks into smaller ones, which are easier to accomplish. Items you will probably put on your list include:

► writing or updating your resume
► getting your resume printed
► purchasing outfits to wear to interviews
► following up with interviewers post-interview

Once your list is complete, write down how long you think each task will take to accomplish.

Next, prioritize your list. Determine what tasks need to be done immediately, and which items can wait until later in the job search process. When you know what needs to be done and approximately how long it will take to accomplish each task, create a schedule for yourself and set deadlines.

Using your personal planner, calendar, or PDA, start at today's date and enter in each job search-related task, one at a time. Under your list of tasks to complete, add items like "check the help wanted ads" and "update resume." Leave yourself enough time to accomplish each task, and in your planner, mark down the date by which each task should be completed.

Keep meticulous notes in your planner or on your PDA. Write down everything you do, with whom you make contact, the phone numbers and addresses of your contacts, topics of discussion on the phone or during interviews, the follow-up actions that need to be taken, and even what you wore to each interview. Throughout your job search process, keep your planner or PDA with you at all times. Refer to it and update it often to ensure that you remain on track.

Refer to your planner or PDA during job interviews, and don't be afraid to jot down notes during the interview. If the interviewer wants to meet with you again, take out your planner or PDA, and make the appointment on the spot. Not only will you be organized but you will also demonstrate this important quality to a potential employer.

RESEARCHING THE FIELD

Finding the right job always begins with research. You need to know exactly what administrative assistant jobs you're qualified to fill, what jobs are available, where the jobs can be found, and how to land one of those jobs. As mentioned in previous chapters, administrative assistants are employed in just about every setting you can think of, from retail stores to schools, prisons to corporate legal departments. While it's not possible to cover every possible job environment, this chapter covers four of the major employers of administrative assistants: corporations and small businesses, law firms, medical offices, and government agencies, along with resources for finding the information you will want to have about a potential employer, including:

▶ amount of pay and quality of benefits compared to market norms
▶ level of formality and flexibility in the workplace culture
▶ whether there are training programs available to help employees upgrade their skills
▶ promotion, raise policies, and track records
▶ level of family friendliness (flex time for children's doctor's visits, whether childcare facilities are available on the premises, and so forth)

▶ substantiated complaints against the company

▶ awards won by the company

While doing your research, keep the following questions in mind:

1. What is the organization's financial condition? If you're interested in a for-profit concern, information on growth prospects for the industry that the company represents is important.

2. Is the organization's business or activity in keeping with your own interests and ethics? It is easier and more pleasant to go to work if you are enthusiastic about what the organization does.

3. How will the size of the organization affect you? Large firms generally offer a greater variety of training programs and career paths, more levels to advance to, and better employee benefits than small firms. Large employers may also have better facilities and equipment. However, jobs in large companies are often very specialized, whereas jobs in small companies may offer more variety and responsibility, a closer working relationship with management, and a chance to see your contribution to the success of the organization.

4. Should you work for a new small company or organization or for one that is well established? New small businesses have a high failure rate, but for many people, the excitement of getting in on the ground floor and helping to create the business or organization, and the potential for sharing in its success, makes up for the risk of job loss.

5. Is the organization in an industry with favorable long-term prospects? The most successful firms tend to be in industries that are growing rapidly.

6. Where is the job located? If it is in another city, is the cost of living higher than you're used to? What about the availability of housing and transportation, and the quality of educational and recreational facilities in the new location? Will there be excessive commuting time?

Corporations and Small Businesses

The easiest way to get background information on a company is to contact the company itself. Try telephoning its public relations office and asking for information. You may receive a copy of the company's annual report to the stockholders, which describes its corporate philosophy, history, products or services, goals, and financial status. Press releases, company newsletters or magazines, and recruitment brochures also can be helpful.

Background information on the organization also may be available at your public or school library. If you cannot get an annual report, check the library for reference directories that provide basic facts about the company, such as earnings, products and services, and number of employees. Some directories that are widely available in libraries include the following:

- ▶ Dun & Bradstreet's Million Dollar Directory
- ▶ Standard and Poor's Register of Corporations
- ▶ Directors and Executives
- ▶ Moody's Industrial Manual
- ▶ Thomas' Register of American Manufacturers
- ▶ Ward's Business Directory

The Internet is also an excellent resource for researching potential employers. Below are listed a number of sites that may be useful in finding the information you're looking for.

www.analysiszone.com
www.businessjeeves.com/MoneyComInd.html
www.corporateinformation.com
www.companydescriptions.com
www.planetbiz.com

Don't forget to check with your school's placement office, which should also have information about nearby corporations that employ administrative assistants. They may even have valuable contacts with companies that routinely hire their graduates.

Law Firms

The *Martindale-Hubbell Law Directory* is a multi-volume set that includes the names, addresses, and phone numbers of all lawyers and law firms in the U. S. This information is listed by attorney name, firm name, location, and specialty. The directory also lists lawyers employed by corporations and governments. If your placement office doesn't have a copy, check the nearest law library. You can also access Martindale-Hubbell on the Web at www.martindale.com. West Publishing also maintains an Internet directory of attorneys, called West's Legal Directory, at www.wld.com.

Your state, county, or city bar association also compiles a directory of attorneys. In most cases, it will list the lawyers by name and by area of practice. And don't overlook the phone book as a resource. Most Yellow Pages have a section for attorneys or lawyers that includes lists by practice area as well as alphabetical lists.

The Healthcare Industry

The healthcare industry is booming, and along with it the administrative tasks are growing as well. You will find many job opportunities not only in doctors' offices but in hospitals, laboratories, HMOs, and other medical related workplaces. If you have specialized in medical skills, check with your school's placement office and your instructors for information about local firms and offices that may be hiring. For a more general look at the industry, search the Internet with terms such as "administrative assistant" and "healthcare" or "medical."

There are also field-specific sites aimed at those looking to get into the health field. Many magazines and journals for the industry are online, and websites that advertise jobs, such as Medical Employment Services (www.ppservice.com), Medical and Healthcare Jobs Page (www.nationjob. com/medical/), and Monster Healthcare (www.medsearch.com), are worth exploring. Some hospitals and companies also have Web pages that list job openings, such as www.medctr.ucla.edu/ (UCLA Medical Center) and www. reidhosp.com (Reid Hospital and Health Care Services in Richmond, Indiana).

Government Agencies

There are thousands of administrative assistant jobs within the government at the federal, state, and municipal levels. In order to find out more about the positions available, you will need to decide which departments or agencies you're interested in. All of them require the services of administrative assistants. At the federal level, each department has its own website where you can find more information about the type of work they do. Contacts will also be listed so you can continue your research if a particular agency interest you. For a list of federal government agencies, with links to their sites, log onto www.lib.lsu.edu/gov/fedgovall.html.

Government Positions

All you need for an administrative career with the federal government is a high school diploma (or GED) and U.S. citizenship. For some clerical jobs, you will also be required to take the Federal Clerical and Administrative Support Exam. This test assesses math and verbal skills, as well as typing proficiency. Clerical and administrative support is a broad description of a job whose exact responsibilities can vary greatly depending on the agency you work for. In general, support personnel assist higher-level employees by performing such tasks as:

- answering telephones
- typing correspondence
- working with mail and files
- doing data entry
- performing stenography (taking dictation) by hand or on a machine

Not all federal jobs require that you take the Clerical and Administrative Support Exam. Agencies may also hire based on interviews, work samples or experience. For a complete listing of available federal jobs, visit the U.S. Office of Personnel Management's website at www.usajobs.opm.gov. For help preparing for the Clerical and Administrative Support Exam, look for LearningExpress's *Federal Clerical Exam Test Preparation Guide.*

For government positions at the state level, check with your State Job Service office. A list of these offices may be found at jobsearch.about.com/library/blstatedol.htm. Also, check the section on page 105 entitled

"Government Job Searches" for more ideas about how to find out about administrative assistant jobs with the government.

FINDING THE JOBS AVAILABLE

There are a number of great ways to locate employment as an administrative assistant. Some have been around for years, such as classified ads and job placement firms. Others are more recent additions to the job search arena and offer great possibilities. They include such Internet resources as industry-specific sites, some of which list employment opportunities, and general career-related websites.

School Career Placement Centers

Almost every school has a career placement center, whose director has the job of helping you find employment when you graduate. A good placement office will have directories of businesses in the local area, information about job fairs, and copies of any industry publications that list administrative assistant job openings. A top placement director also maintains contacts with the business community so that your school's placement office will be one of the first places to hear about a job opening and can give you valuable general information about the market in your area.

Temporary Agencies

As mentioned in Chapter 1, temping is an excellent job-search method. Temporary agencies can open the door not only to short-term employment, but to full-time work as well. You can also gain some real world experience, improve your skills with interactive computer training programs, and learn tips on the proper protocol for doing office work.

Kelly Services has a program called KellySelect, a temporary-to-hire service that lets employers evaluate a candidate's performance during a 90-day trial assignment before making a hiring decision. While at work during the 90 days, the worker receives excellent on-the-job training. The employer has the option, as well, of hiring the candidate immediately if he or she appears especially qualified. KellySelect is also a direct placement service. An employer contracts with Kelly Services to find a candidate for a particular job. Kelly then acts as a kind of human resources agency for that employer, finding a candidate that meets that employer's needs for direct hire.

For some, what starts as a job search strategy becomes full-time temporary employment. These administrative assistants love the variety of assignments and changes in work environments that temping provides. In addition, many temporary agencies now offer benefits to go along with the flexibility inherent in the work. In Chapter 1 you heard from Byron and Valerie Demmer, who have enjoyed 15 years of temporary office work while traveling and pursuing outside interests. Temporary office professional Henry Shapiro, who has done temporary administrative work through a staffing agency for seven years, agrees:

> I got my degree in art history. After graduation, I had initially planned to find an administrative job in the museum field, and I started temping so that I'd have a steady source of income while I was job-hunting. But I found that I really liked the freedom that temporary work gave me. I've worked for all kinds of companies in all kinds of environments, and it's been interesting to work with so many different people. The fast pace of my work, and the frequent changes, keep it from ever getting monotonous.

JUST THE FACTS

According to a 2001 report from the American Staffing Association (ASA), as many as 12.5 million people worked with temporary staffing firms in 2000. ASA's analysis of data from the Bureau of Labor Statistics indicates that "temporary employees are more likely to be better educated, higher paid, and prefer the flexibility of temporary employment than their shorter-term counterparts." The report also notes that "while most people choose temporary employment as a bridge to a permanent job, about one-third of temporary employees prefer the arrangement and choose it for longer periods."

Source: "Scaling New Heights: ASA's Annual Analysis of the Staffing Industry." American Staffing Association, May 2001.

Available at http://staffingtoday.net/staffstats/annualanalysis01.pdf

Classified Ads

Conventional job-hunting wisdom says you shouldn't depend too much on want ads for finding a job. However, this resource shouldn't be overlooked, especially if you're still in school. By reading the classifieds, you can learn valuable information about the market for administrative assistants in your area. For instance, you will see at least a partial list of the places that hire administrative assistants.

You can also get an idea of typical salaries and benefits in your area. Since one of the hardest questions to answer on an application or in an interview is "What is your desired salary?" it can be worthwhile to watch the ads and know the going rate ahead of time. You can also get information about temporary and part-time jobs, which are very common ways for administrative assistants to begin their careers.

Aside from the educational aspect of want ads, reading and responding to them may actually lead to a position. Many companies advertise administrative assistant positions this way, primarily because it is an inexpensive way to reach a large number of potential applicants. However, that means that, depending on your area, dozens of applicants will send a resume to the employer, and you will be competing with all of them. Don't wait to respond. If the ad appears in the Sunday newspaper, respond to it on Monday morning. Used properly, classifieds can not only improve your knowledge of the job market, but they can lead to your first position as a administrative assistant.

Job Directories

While the Internet has probably surpassed the library in terms of usefulness in your job search, your local library and chamber of commerce are also good places to look. Both maintain directories of employers in your area. Two excellent sources organized specifically for job hunters are *The World Almanac National Job Finder's Guide* (St. Martin's Press) and the *Job Bank series* (Adams, Inc.). There are brief job descriptions and online resources in the *Job Finder's Guide*; *Job Bank* books are published by geographic region and contain a section profiling specific companies, with contact information for major employers in your region sorted by industry. Once you've identified companies in your area of interest, use the resources at your local library to learn more about them. Your librarian can help you find public information about local businesses, including the names of all the company's officers, the number of employees, a brief description of the company, and contact information.

Employment or Personnel Agencies

Employment agencies search for full-time employment opportunities for you. Be sure to find out who is responsible for paying the fee before you sign up with an agency; some charge it to you, while others collect it from your new employer. After you are placed in a job, your relationship with the placement agency ends. To find job placement firms in your area, search the Internet with the terms "employment agency and administrative assistant."

Job Fairs

Attending job or career fairs is another way to find employment. Job fairs bring together a number of employers under one roof, usually at a hotel, convention center, or civic center. These employers send representatives to the fair to inform prospective employees about their company, accept resumes, and, occasionally, to conduct interviews for open positions. Many fairs are held specifically for administrative assistant employers and prospective employees. They usually hold seminars for attendees covering such topics as resume writing, job hunting strategies, and interviewing skills. To find the next scheduled job fair in your area, contact the information office of the convention center or civic center nearest you and ask if there's a job fair is on their upcoming events calendar. The local newspaper or state unemployment office may have relevant information. And check the Internet with the search terms "job fair and administrative assistant."

While it's true that you will most likely be competing with many other job seekers at a job fair, your ability to impress an employer is far greater during an in-person meeting than it is if you simply respond to a help wanted ad by submitting your resume. By attending a job fair, your appearance, level of preparation, what you say and how you say it, and your body language can be used to help make an employer interested in hiring you. When attending a job fair, your goal is to get invited to come in later for a formal in-person interview. Since you will have limited time with an employer at a job fair, typically between five and ten minutes, it's very rare that an employer will hire someone on the spot, but this does happen.

Preparation on your part is vital. Determine beforehand which employers will be there and whether or not you have the qualifications to fill the job openings available. Begin your research by visiting the website created to promote the job fair you are interested in attending. The website typically lists detailed information about the firms attending and what types of jobs participating employers are looking to fill. Once you pinpoint the firms you're interested in, research them as if you're preparing for an actual in-person job interview.

Determine exactly how your qualifications and skills meet the needs of employers in which you are interested. Also, develop a list of questions to ask the employer during your in-person meeting at the job fair. Showing a sincere interest in working for an employer and asking questions that demonstrate your interest will help set you apart from the competition in a positive way.

Bring plenty of copies of your resume to the job fair. Begin your visit to the job fair by visiting the companies you're most interested in working for. It's best to visit these firms as early in the day as possible, since as the day goes on, the people working the job fair tend to get tired and may be less responsive, especially if they've already met with several dozen potential applicants. You should be prepared to answer questions about why you want to work for that firm and how your skills and qualifications make you qualified to fill one of the positions the employer has available. As you meet with people, collect business cards and follow up your meetings later that day with a short letter, e-mail, or fax thanking the person you met with for their time. Use this correspondence to reaffirm your interest in working for an employer.

Online Resources

As mentioned before in this chapter, one of the fastest growing and most comprehensive resources for job searching is the Internet. Next, two types of sites that you should find to be of great use as you look for employment are featured. The first, career-related websites, offer help with every step of the process, from resume writing to researching a firm before accepting a job offer. You may also network with other people in your field, and obtain valuable career-related advice on some of these sites. The second type of site is geared toward administrative or support staff, and contains lists of job openings geared specifically to your profession.

Career-Related Websites

The following are some of the online resources available to the job hunter. But don't limit yourself to this selection; using any Internet Search Engine or portal, you can enter a keyword such as: "resume," "job," "career," "job listings," or "help wanted" to find thousands of others. You can also perform a keyword search using "administrative assistant."

6-Figure Jobs—www.6figurejobs.com
About.com—jobsearch.about.com/cs/resumes
America's Employers—www.americasemployers.com
America's Job Bank—www.ajb.dni.us
Best Jobs USA—www.bestjobsusa.com
Boston Herald's Job Find—www.jobfind.com
Career Builder—www.careerbuilder.com
Career Center—www.jobweb.org/catapult/guenov/res.html#explore
Career Spectrum—www.careerspectrum.com/dir-resume.htm
Career.com—www.career.com
CareerMosaic—www.careermosaic.com
CareerNet—www.careers.org
CareerWeb—www.cweb.com
College Central Network—www.employercentral.com
Gary Will's Worksearch—www.garywill.com/worksearch
JobBank USA—www.jobbankusa.com
JobLynx—www.joblynx.com

JobSource—www.jobsource.com

JobStar—www.jobsmart.org/tools/resume

Monster—www.monster.com

Occupational Outlook Handbook—www.stats.bls.gov

Quintessential Careers—www.quintcareers.com/resres.html

Salary.com—www.salary.com

Taos Careers—www.taos.com/resumetips.html

Vault.com—www.vault.com/

Wall Street Journal Careers—www.careers.wsj.com

Yahoo Careers—careers.yahoo.com

Administrative Assistant Employment Sites

Most of these sites list only jobs in your profession; however, a few of them are more comprehensive. Use the search term "administrative assistant" to come up with a list of only those job openings that will be of interest to you.

AdminConnection—www.adminconnection.com

AdminExchange—www.adminexchange.com

America's Job Bank (The Public Employment Service)—www.ajb.dni.us

*CareerPath—www.careerpath.com

Federal Job Announcements—www.fedworld.gov/jobs/jobsearch.html

4Temps—www.4temps.com

Job Administrator—www.jobadministrator.net

Job Science—www.jobmedicalsupport.com

Kelly Services—www.kellyservices.com

Manpower, Inc.—www.manpower.com

Nonprofit Job Resource Center—www.nonprofitcareer.com

Public Service Jobs—www.umich.edu/academic/opsp/jobsalert

Secretary Job Store—www.secretaryjobstore.com

Snelling Personnel Services—www.snelling.com

*CareerPath lists ads from major newspapers, including the *Boston Globe, Chicago Tribune, Los Angeles Times, New York Times, San Jose Mercury News, Washington Post, Philadelphia Inquirer*, and *Southern Florida Sun-Sentinel*.

Government Job Searches

Finding a job with the government is a more involved process than finding one at a small business or corporation. While some federal agencies have the authority to test and hire applicants directly, most work through the Office of Personnel Management (OPM), which accepts applications, administers the appropriate written tests, and then submits an eligibility list of qualified candidates to the agency for consideration. For example, if you want a job with the Bureau of Alcohol, Tobacco, and Firearms (ATF), you will have to wait until you see a specific vacancy announcement posted through the OPM, then go through the office to start the application process.

There are several ways to get information from OPM, with the easiest being through their website at www.opm.gov. On this site, you can read answers to frequently asked questions, read about changes that are affecting government employees, read, and download or print some of the forms you may need, and get some background information about the OPM. You can also contact them at 912-757-3000, TDD 912-744-2299, or by modem at 912-757-3100.

The OPM also operates www.usajobs.opm.gov, which lists employment opportunities, including the full text of the job announcement. The announcement will give you the classification of the job, known as a grade. It will indicate the experience necessary, salary level, and other features. Once you have read the application process for a specific job, you can access an online application that may be used to create a resume. After creating it, you can submit the resume electronically, or save it to their system to retrieve and edit for future use.

You may also find an administrative assistant position with the government at many individual government agencies, which do their own hiring and maintain websites that list job openings.

These agencies include the Federal Aviation Administration (jobs.faa. gov), the Department of Housing and Urban Development (www.hud.gov/jobs), and the Internal Revenue Service (www.irs.gov/hot/employment/index.html), among many others.

Federal Jobs Digest maintains a website that claims to be the country's premier source of federal job information. They not only post job openings, but also allow you to register your resume, conduct a job-matching search, and read job descriptions, including the extensive benefits that come with federal employment. Check them out at www.jobsfed.com.

Industry-specific periodicals, such as those listed later in this section, often list federal government job openings, as do national newspapers. If the federal job is in a local area, such as the local office of the Federal Bureau of Investigation, it may be listed in a local newspaper. You may also get information from a Federal Job Information Center. There is at least one of these centers in each state, which posts federal job openings for the area in which it is located. While many offer only a recording over the telephone or several job announcements posted on the wall, they can be a worthwhile contact.

Industry Newsletters and Magazines

Knowing how to stay on top of changes in the field in which you're working will help make you a more attractive candidate for any job. One of the best ways to track changes and identify trends is by reading newspapers and publications geared toward the field. These publications will announce breaking news and explain its significance. Being up on industry news will help convince potential employers that you will be a valuable asset.

If you're already a member of one or more of the administrative assistant associations, you're familiar with the publications they produce (the Administrative Resource Network, Admin Authority, and International Association of Administrative Professionals all publish newsletters online). If not, they are listed in Appendix B. You will also want to keep up with the industry in which you're working. For instance, if you're employed in the legal field, check out newsletters put out by your state bar association; medical secretaries may want to read up on advances in their field by perusing journals published by the American Medical Association, and online newsletters. Your Internet search skills will be of great use in finding pertinent news and information.

NETWORKING

The authors of the *Complete Office Handbook*, a publication of Professional Secretaries International, write: "It is estimated that up to 90 percent of jobs are filled by word of mouth." They're referring to networking, making contact with others to obtain information or get help meeting a specific goal. But no matter how widespread and important its use, networking remains intimidating to some, who picture it as insincere small talk or handshaking. However, when it is done properly, it is completely sincere and can provide many benefits, such as:

▶ mentoring
▶ making contacts within a hiring firm or company
▶ furthering training
▶ getting information about trends in the industry

The key to successful networking is to break down the process into easy-to-follow steps. These steps are explored in the next section, which shows each step as it is directly applied to an administrative assistant job search.

Step One: Identify Small Goals

Of course your ultimate goal, not only for networking, but for the entire job search process, is to find a great job. However, you shouldn't approach day-to-day networking as a means to that larger goal. Instead, as your first step, identify smaller goals that can be met quickly. For instance, you have narrowed down your search to three companies in your area. Now, you want to get inside information about these offices in order to decide where to apply for a job. Or, you may simply be seeking advice from those already working in the field. Once your goals are identified, you can best determine how to meet them.

Step Two: Be Informed

If your goal is to seek advice about corporations in your area, get as much information as you can first. Research the companies that hire administrative assistants as described earlier. Understand the field in general, too. You want to sound like you have done your homework when you begin to make contacts.

This is also the step in which you begin to make a list of potential contacts that may help you meet your goal(s). If you're in school, the person at the job placement office should be at the head of your list. Then, look to your research: you've probably read the names of others you can add to your list (heads of human resource departments, and others who do the hiring for their companies). Others who may be of help to you are:

▶ friends and relatives
▶ current or past coworkers or fellow students
▶ former teachers
▶ people you meet at meetings or at parties
▶ the insurance salesperson who comes to call
▶ secretaries at various offices you may visit on personal business
▶ people who work for a company you'd like to work for (the *Complete Office Handbook* recommends finding out where such people go for lunch or after work, although it doesn't tell how to start a conversation with them—perhaps you can think of a creative way)
▶ people you meet on jobs you get through a temporary agency

Newsletters from your administrative assistant associations may list administrative assistants working in your area. The students and teachers you met during your training are also good candidates for this list.

Step Three: Make a Connection

Using the list of potential contacts you developed in Step Two, build a network of administrative assistants who work at the offices you are interested in joining. Call them or visit their offices. Although busy, most will take a few minutes to speak with a prospective newcomer. They were new to the business once themselves, so if you are careful not to take up too much of their time, they will probably be willing to give you some information. Begin by introducing yourself, showing that you are informed (Step Two) and interested in what they have to say. Then, ask if they are willing to help you.

Step Four: Ask for What You Want

If your contact indicates that he or she is willing to help you, be honest and direct about what you want. If your goal is to find out inside information about the office in which a contact works, tell her that you are thinking of applying to work there. Then, ask questions such as:

- ▶ "How do you like the office?"
- ▶ "What are the benefits of working here?"
- ▶ "What is the office atmosphere like?"
- ▶ "Where else have you worked, and how does this office compare?"

Step Five: Expand Your Network

One of the most valuable pieces of information you can get from a contact is another contact. After you've gotten the information you need to meet your Step One goal(s), simply ask if he or she would mind sharing with you the name of another person who might also be able to help you.

Also consider requesting informational interviews at firms that interest you. An informational interview is one in which you meet with someone to find out about the company. It may be an excellent opportunity to:

- ▶ learn more about how the firm works
- ▶ gain interview experience
- ▶ make a contact that might help you get a job in the future

You can also expand your circle of contacts by joining professional organizations while you're still a student (the International Association of Administrative Professionals even offers a discounted student membership). Be sure to join both national organizations and their local chapters. Though the national organizations can give you valuable information, it's on the local level that you will be more effective at networking. Go to local meetings and ask questions—people almost always like to talk about their jobs—and volunteer for committees. The members of your local administrative assistant group will most likely know about job openings before anyone else does.

Step Six: Organize Yourself

It's likely that you already have written down your goals and made lists of contacts. Once you've spoken with some of them, organization becomes even more important. You will need to keep track of your contacts, as well as the information you receive from them. When you need to connect with this person again in the future, you will be able to easily access your information. There are software packages that can help you to keep track of your networking contacts, or, you can simply use a notebook and organize yourself. For each contact, note:

- ▶ name
- ▶ address
- ▶ e-mail address
- ▶ phone number (work, pager, cellular phone, residence)
- ▶ fax number
- ▶ company name
- ▶ job title
- ▶ first meeting—where, when, the topics you discussed
- ▶ last contact—when, why, and how

Step Seven: Maintain Your Contacts

It is important to maintain your contacts once you have established them. Try to reach people again within a couple of weeks of meeting them. You can send a note of thanks, ask a question, or send a piece of information related to your conversation with them. This contact cements your meeting in their minds so they will remember you more readily when you call them again in the future. If you haven't communicated with your contacts for a few months, you might send them a note or e-mail about an article you read, relevant new technology, or other information, to keep your name fresh in their minds.

As you begin your job hunt, keep in mind that you are not just looking for a job; you're looking for a good job, one you will enjoy and feel challenged by. Once you've finished your training, you will be ready for such a job and you will have a lot to offer to any employer. Remember: you're not begging for employment; you're trying to find an employer who will be a match for your skills and talents.

THE INSIDE TRACK

Who: Jessica Namakkal
What: Membership & Development Assistant
Where: UCLA Hammer Museum of Art & Cultural Center

INSIDER'S STORY

I work in two departments in an art museum on a college campus. I process memberships: collect money, run credit cards, enter information into the member database, generate membership packets and send information out to new members. I also maintain a database for the Development Department and process incoming gifts. Sometimes I am involved in researching companies and foundations as potential donors, and working on low-level grant proposals. I make and distribute the development report and membership rosters on a weekly basis. I work about 40 hours per week.

I have a B.A. in history from the University of Southern California. I didn't plan to go into administrative work after graduation, but I discovered that administrative jobs are often open to people at the entry level and offer competitive salaries. I think a bachelor's degree in the humanities or social sciences is good preparation for these types of jobs.

I found this job through a friend of my previous boss. I think that internships, or other experience in the field, and having contacts are the most important elements of looking for a job.

I've only been here for a few months, but I'd definitely like to stay in my current position. I enjoy the people I work with, and have found that working with interesting people makes the work far more exciting. Also, if I decide that I really want to work in museums and with arts, then I am in the right place and could move beyond my current position. In my experience, computer skills are absolutely the most important thing for someone entering this field. While I didn't go to school for administrative training, I find that I'm a lot more comfortable with computers than many of the people I work with. Knowing how to use a database, in particular, has been a real asset.

CHAPTER five

JOB SEARCH SKILLS

Once you have pinpointed the job opportunities you're interested in pursuing, you will need to contact your potential employer to express your interest. The way you accomplish that contact can be just as important as your skills and training. This chapter will provide you with the advice you need to ensure that the impression you leave is the very best possible, making you can stand out as a superior candidate. Then, once you receive a job offer or offers, you will need to evaluate them and make a decision. Useful tips are included on how to go about this final step on your path to employment.

YOUR FIRST contact with a potential employer may be through a phone call, a mailed cover letter and resume, an e-mailed resume, or an interview. Whatever the form, it is imperative that you use it to make an excellent impression. A resume containing spelling errors, an unprofessional sounding phone call, or an interview to which you arrive ten minutes late can all mean disaster to a job search. Once you're offered a job, you will need to handle the offer professionally, too.

It's not hard to master the job search skills you need to succeed, but it does take some time and effort. By carefully reading this chapter, you will learn how to land the job you want by writing great cover letters and resumes, interviewing with confidence and proficiency, and assessing job offers thoroughly and honestly.

WRITING YOUR RESUME

Whether you are responding to an advertisement, following up on a net-working opportunity, or making a cold contact, your resume is usually the first means by which a potential employer learns about you. Think of it as an advertisement you write to help sell yourself. A successful advertisement catches your attention by combining several elements: content, composition, clarity, and concentration. Falling short in any of these areas can cause a reader to pass over the ad; you want to make sure that a prospective employer will pay attention to yours.

As you write, edit, and proofread your resume, make an effort to keep all of the information short, to the point, and totally relevant. Anything you leave out can be discussed later, during a job interview. The purpose of your resume is to get an employer interested enough in you so you make it to the next level, getting invited for an interview.

Creating a powerful resume will take time and effort. Even if you have written dozens before, it is worth your while to seek out good resume-writing resources to help you draft one for your new career as an administrative assistant. While much has remained the same over the years, there are current standards and trends for resumes, including e-mailed and computer scannable resumes, that you should know about. To start, check out your school's placement office, which may have copies of former students' resumes. Books such as *Great Resume* by Jason R. Rich (LearningExpress, 2000) contain excellent general guidelines. And there are plenty of online resources to help you create a winning resume, including the following:

Damn Good Resume: www.damngood.com/jobseekers/tips.htm
The Elegant Resume: resumeadvice.tripod.com
e Resume Writing: www.eresumewriting.com
JobStar: www.jobstar.org/tools/resume
JobWeb: www.jobweb.com/catapult/guenov/restips.html
Learn 2 Write A Resume: www.learn2.com/07/0768/0768.asp
Monster.com Resume Center: resume.monster.com
Rebecca Smith's eResumes & Resources—www.eresumes.com
Resumania—www.resumania.com
Resume Magic—www.liglobal.com/b_c/career/res.shtml

Resume Tutor: www1.umn.edu/ohr/ocep/resume
Resume Workshop owl.english.purdue.edu/workshops/hypertext/
    Resumew/index.html
10 Minute Resume: www.10minuteresume.com

The next topic is the four elements of resume writing: content, composition, clarity, and concentration.

Content

Use the following questionnaire to gather the information you will need for your resume. In the following sections, we'll cover how best to organize, format, and word it to make the best possible impression.

Contact Information

The only personal information that belongs on your resume is your name (on every page, if your resume exceeds one page in length), address, phone number, and fax number and e-mail address if you have them. Under no circumstances should you include personal information such as age, gender, religion, health or marital status, or number of children.

Full name:_____
Permanent Street Address:_____
City, State, Zip:_____
Daytime Telephone Number:_____
Evening Telephone Number:_____
Pager/Cell Phone Number (Optional):_____
Fax Number (Optional):_____
E-Mail Address:_____
Personal Website Address/Online Portfolio URL:_____
School Address (if applicable):_____
Your Phone Number at School (if applicable):_____

Job/Career Objective(s)

Write a short description of the job you're seeking. Be sure to include as much information as possible about how you can use your skills to the employer's benefit. Later, you will condense this answer into one short sentence.

_____

_____

_____

_____

What is the job title you're looking to fill? _____

_____

Educational Background

Be sure to include your internship in this section. For many recent graduates, it is their only office experience, and perhaps their only work experience. Include the skills you learned which will be applicable to the position for which you're applying.

List the most recent college or university you have attended: _____

City/State: _____

What year did you start?: _____

Graduation month/year: _____

Degree(s) and/or award(s) earned: _____

Your major: _____

Your minor(s): _____

List some of your most impressive accomplishments, extracurricular activities, club affiliations, etc.: _____

_____

List computer courses you've taken that help qualify you for the job you're

seeking: _____

_____

_____

Grade point average (GPA): _____

Other college/university you have attended: _____

City/State: _____

What year did you start?: _____

Graduation month/year: _____

Degree(s) and/or award(s) earned: _____

Your major: _____

Your minor(s): _____

List some of your most impressive accomplishments, extracurricular activities, club affiliations, etc.: _____

_____

_____

List computer courses you've taken that help qualify you for the job you're seeking: _____

_____

_____

Grade point average (GPA): _____

High school attended: _____

City/State: _____

Graduation date: _____

Grade point average (GPA): _____

List the names and phone numbers of one or two current or past professors/teachers (or guidance counselors) you can contact about obtaining a letter of recommendation or list as a reference: _____

_____

_____

_____

Personal Skills & Abilities

Your personal skill set (the combination of skills you possess) is something that differentiates you from everyone else. Skills that are marketable in the workplace aren't always taught in school, however. Your ability to manage people, stay cool under pressure, remain organized, surf the Internet, use software applications, speak in public, communicate well in writing, communicate in multiple languages, or perform research, are all examples of marketable skills.

When reading job descriptions or help wanted ads, pay careful attention to the wording used to describe what the employer is looking for. As you customize your resume for a specific employer, you will want to match up what the employer is looking for with your own qualifications as closely as possible. Try to utilize the wording provided by the employer within the classified ad or job description.

What do you believe is your most marketable skill? Why? _____

_____

_____

_____

List three or four specific examples of how you have used this skill in the past while at work. What was accomplished as a result?

1. _____
2. _____
3. _____
4. _____

What are keywords or buzzwords that can be used to describe your skill? _____

_____

_____

_____

What is another of your marketable skills? _____

_____

_____

_____

Provide at least three examples of how you've used this skill in the workplace:

1. _____
2. _____
3. _____

What unusual or unique skill(s) do you possess that help you stand out from other applicants applying for the same types of positions as you?

_____

_____

_____

How have you already proven this skill is useful in the workplace?

_____

What computer skills do you possess? _____

_____

What computer software packages are you proficient in (such as Microsoft Office—Word, Excel, PowerPoint, FrontPage, etc.)? _____

_____

Thinking carefully, what skills do you believe you currently lack?

_____

_____

_____

What skills do you have, but that need to be polished or enhanced in order to make you a more appealing candidate? _____

_____

_____

What options are available to you to either obtain or brush up on the skills you believe need improvement (for example: evening/weekend classes at a college or university, adult education classes, seminars, books, home study courses, on-the-job-training, etc.): _____

_____

_____

In what time frame could you realistically obtain this training?

_____

_____

Work/Employment History

Previous work experience is very important. Even if it had nothing to do with your chosen field, every job taught you something that will make you a better administrative assistant. Experience in other fields such as medicine, accounting, real estate, human resources, and insurance, is considered a hiring plus by potential employers. Don't overlook or discount volunteer work for the same reason. You gained skills and experience, and your volunteering also indicates that you are committed to your community. (Keep this in mind as you go through your training; if you are short on experience, you might think about volunteering.)

Complete the employment-related questions that follow for all of your previous employers, including part-time or summer jobs held while in school, as well as temp jobs, internships, and volunteering. You probably won't want to reveal your past earning history to a potential employer, but you may want this information available as reference when you begin negotiating your future salary, benefits, and overall compensation package.

Most recent employer: _____

City, State: _____

Year you began work: _____

Year you stopped working (write "Present" if still employed): _____

Job title: _____

Job description: _____

_____

_____

_____

Reason for leaving: _____

_____

_____

What were your three proudest accomplishments while holding this job?

   1. _____

   2. _____

   3. _____

Contact person at the company who can provide a reference: _____

_____

Contact person's phone number: _____

Annual salary earned: _____

Employer: _____

City, State: _____

Year you began work: _____

Year you stopped working (write "Present" if still employed): _____

Job title: _____

Job description: _____

_____

_____

_____

Reason for leaving: _____

_____

_____

What were your three proudest accomplishments while holding this job?

   1. _____

   2. _____

   3. _____

Contact person at the company who can provide a reference: _____

_____

Contact person's phone number: _____

Annual salary earned: _____

Military Service (if applicable)

Branch of service you served in: _____

Years served: _____

Highest rank achieved: _____

Decorations or awards earned: _____

Special skills or training you obtained: _____

Professional Accreditations and Licenses

List any and all of the professional accreditations and/or licenses you have earned thus far in your career. Be sure to highlight items that directly relate to the job(s) you will be applying for:

_____

_____

Hobbies and Special Interests

You may have life experience that should be emphasized for potential employers. Did you help a spouse in a business? Were you a candidate for public office? Any number of experiences can add to your attractiveness as a job candidate. If you don't have a great deal of work experience, this part of your resume is very important. Think about the things you have done. Which have taught you lessons that are valuable for an administrative assistant to know? If you can't find a way to include those experiences on your resume, mention them in your cover letter.

List any hobbies or special interests you have that are not necessarily work-related, but that potentially could separate you from the competition. Can any of the skills utilized in your hobby be adapted for the workplace?

_____

_____

What non-professional clubs or organizations do you belong to or actively participate in?

_____

_____

Personal/Professional Ambitions

You may not want to share these on your resume, but answering the questions below will help you to focus your search, and prepare for possible interviewing topics.

What are your long-term goals?

Personal: _____

_____

_____

_____

Professional: _____

_____

_____

_____

Financial: _____

_____

_____

_____

For your personal, professional, and then financial goals, what are five smaller, short-term goals you can begin working toward achieving right now that will help you ultimately achieve each of your long-term goals?

Short-term personal goals:

1. _____
2. _____
3. _____
4. _____
5. _____

Short-term professional goals:

1. _____
2. _____
3. _____
4. _____
5. _____

Short-term financial goals:

1. _____
2. _____
3. _____

4._____

5._____

Will the job(s) you will be applying for help you achieve your long-term goals and objectives? If *yes*, how? If *no*, why not?_____

_____

_____

_____

Describe your personal, professional, and financial situation right now:

_____

_____

_____

What would you most like to improve about your life overall?_____

_____

_____

_____

What are a few things you can do, starting immediately, to bring about positive changes in your personal, professional, or financial life?_____

_____

_____

_____

Where would you like to be personally, professionally, and financially five and ten years down the road?_____

_____

_____

_____

What needs to be done to achieve these long-term goals or objectives?

_____

_____

_____

_____

What are some of the qualities about your personality that you're most proud of?_____

_____

_____

_____

What are some of the qualities about your personality that you believe need improvement? _____

_____

_____

_____

What do others most like about you? _____

_____

_____

_____

What do you think others least like about you? _____

_____

_____

_____

If you decided to pursue additional education, what would you study and why? How would this help you professionally? _____

_____

_____

_____

If you had more free time, what would you spend it doing? _____

_____

_____

_____

List several accomplishments in your personal and professional life that you're most proud of. _____

_____

_____

_____

Why did you choose these things?

1. _____
2. _____
3. _____
4. _____
5. _____

What were your strongest and favorite subjects in school? Is there a way to incorporate these interests into the job(s) or career path you're pursuing?

_____

_____

_____

What do you believe is your biggest weakness? Why wouldn't an employer hire you? _____

_____

_____

_____

What would be the ideal atmosphere for you to work in? Do you prefer a large corporate atmosphere, working at home, or working in a small office?

_____

_____

_____

List five qualities about a new job that would make it the ideal employment opportunity for you:

1. _____
2. _____
3. _____
4. _____
5. _____

What did you like most about the last place you worked? _____

_____

_____

_____

What did you like least about the last place you worked? _____

_____

_____

_____

What work-related tasks are you particularly good at? _____

_____

_____

_____

What type of coworkers would you prefer to have? _____
_____
_____
_____

When it comes to work-related benefits and perks, what's most important to you? _____
_____
_____
_____

When you're recognized for doing a good job at work, how do you like to be rewarded? _____
_____
_____
_____

If you were to write a help wanted ad describing your ideal dream job, what would the ad say? _____
_____
_____
_____

Composition

How your resume looks can be as important as what it says. Potential employers may receive a stack of resumes for one job opening, and they probably spend less than one minute deciding which to review further and which to throw away. If you're applying for a job in a fairly conservative field, such as law, you will want to achieve an overall look that does not stand out, but rather is neat, clean, and within standard resume guidelines. If the job you're after is in a more creative or liberal setting, you may get noticed by being a little different. However, it's always best to err on the side of caution.

Use the tips in the following box to help organize the material you gathered in the questionnaire.

Resume Creation Tips

No matter what type of resume you're putting together, use these tips and strategies to ensure your finished document has the most impact possible when a potential employer reads it.

Always use standard letter-size paper in ivory, cream, or another neutral color.

Include your name, address, and phone number on every page.

Make sure your name is larger than anything else on the page (example: your name in 14-point font, the rest in 12 point).

Use a font that is easy to read, such as 12-point Times New Roman.

Do not use more than three fonts in your resume.

Edit, edit, edit. Read it forward and backward, and then have friends with good proofreading skills read it. Don't rely heavily on grammar and spell checkers, which can miss errors.

Use bullet points for items in a list—they highlight your main points, making them hard to miss.

Use key words in your field.

Avoid using excessive graphics such as boxes, distracting lines, and complex designs.

Be consistent when using bold, capitalization, underlining, and italics. If one company name is underlined, make sure all are underlined. Check titles, dates, et cetera.

Don't list your nationality, race, religion, or gender. Keep your resume as neutral as possible. Your resume is a summary of your skills and abilities.

Don't put anything personal on your resume such as your birth date, marital status, height, or hobbies.

One page is best, but do not crowd your resume. Shorten the margins if you need more space; if it's necessary to create a two-page resume, make sure you balance the information on each page. Don't put just one section on the second page. Be careful about where the page break occurs.

Keep your resume updated. Don't write "9/97 to present" if you ended your job two months ago. Do not cross out or handwrite changes on your resume.

Understand and remember everything written on your resume. Be able to back up all statements with specific examples.

You can organize the information on your resume in a number of ways, depending on your work history, and how the hiring company wants the resume submitted. The three most common formats are:

▶ chronological format
▶ skills format (also known as a functional resume)
▶ combination of chronological and skills format

The most common resume format is chronological—you summarize your work experience year-by-year, beginning with your current or most recent employment experience and working backward. For each job, list the dates you were employed, the name and location of the company for which you worked, and the position(s) you held. Work experience is followed by education, which is also organized chronologically.

The skills resume (also known as the functional resume) emphasizes what you can do rather than what you have done. It is useful if you have large gaps in your work history or have relevant skills that would not be properly highlighted in a chronological listing of jobs. The skills resume concentrates on your skills and qualifications. Specific jobs you have held are listed, but they are not the primary focus of this type of resume.

You may decide a combination of the chronological and skills resume would be best to highlight your skills. A combination resume allows for a mixture of your skills with a chronological list of jobs you have held. You get the best of both resumes. This is an excellent choice for students who have limited work experience and who want to highlight specific skills.

Making Your Resume Computer-Friendly

One of the biggest trends in terms of corporate recruiting is for employers to accept resumes online via e-mail, through one of the career-related websites, or via their own website. If you're going to be applying for jobs online or submitting your resume via e-mail, you will need to create an electronic resume (in addition to a traditional printed resume).

Many companies scan all resumes from job applicants using a computer software program with optical character recognition (OCR), and then enter them into a database, where they can be searched using keywords. When e-mailing your electronic resume directly to an employer, as a general rule, the document should be saved in an ASCII, rich text, or plain text file. Contact the employer directly to see which method is preferred.

When sending a resume via e-mail, the message should begin as a cover letter (and contain the same information as a cover letter). You can then either attach the resume file to the e-mail message or paste the resume text within the message. Be sure to include your e-mail address and well as your regular mailing address and phone number(s) within all e-mail correspondence. Never assume an employer will receive your message and simply hit "respond" using their e-mail software to contact you.

Guidelines for Creating an Electronic Resume to be Saved and Submitted in an ASCII Format

Set the document's left and right margins so that 6.5 inches of text will be displayed per line. This will insure that the text won't automatically wrap to the next line (unless you want it to).

Use a basic, 12-point text font, such as Courier or Times Roman.

Avoid using bullets or other symbols. Instead, use an asterisk (*) or a dash (-). Instead of using the percentage sign (%) for example, spell out the word *percent*.

Use the spell check feature of the software used to create your electronic resume and then proofread the document carefully. Just as applicant tracking software is designed to pick out keywords from your resume that showcase you as a qualified applicant, these same software packages used by employers can also instantly count the number of typos and spelling errors in your document and report that to an employer as well.

Avoid using multiple columns, tables or charts within your document.

Within the text, avoid abbreviations—spell everything out. For example, use the word *Director*, not *Dir.* and use *Vice President* as opposed to *VP*. In terms of degrees, however, it's acceptable to use terms like MBA, B.A., Ph.D., etc.

Use more than one page, if necessary. The computer can handle two or three, and the more skills you list in this extra space, the more hits you will get from the computer (a hit occurs when one of your skills matches what the computer is looking for).

Properly formatting your electronic resume is critical to having is scanned or read properly; however, it's what you say within your resume that will ultimately get you hired. According to Rebecca Smith, M.Ed., author of *Electronic Resumes & Online Networking* (Career Press, 2nd Edition) and companion website (www.eresumes.com), "Keywords are the basis of the electronic search and retrieval process. They provide the context from which to search for a resume in a database, whether the database is a proprietary one that serves a specific purpose, or whether it is a Web-based search engine that serves the general public. Keywords are a tool to quickly browse without having to access the complete text. Keywords are used to identify and retrieve resumes for the user. Employers and recruiters generally search resume databases using keywords: nouns and phrases that highlight technical and professional areas of expertise, industry-related jargon, projects, achievements, special task forces and other distinctive features about a prospect's work history." The emphasis is not on trying to second-guess every possible keyword a recruiter may use to find your resume. Your focus is on selecting and organizing your resume's content in order to highlight those keywords for a variety of online situations. The idea is to identify all possible keywords that are appropriate to your skills and accomplishments that support the kinds of jobs you are looking for. But to do that, you must apply traditional resume writing principles to the concept of extracting those keywords from your resume. Once you have written your resume, then you can identify your strategic keywords based on how you imagine people will search for your resume.

Examples of good keywords are:

Taylor Business Institute
B.A. degree
International Association of Administrative Professionals
Certified Professional Secretary
CPS (the computer will understand acronyms if they are specific to the profession)
French (language fluency)
Chicago (location)
Lotus 1-2-3
spreadsheet software
organized
dependable
responsible
energetic

Industry-related buzzwords, job-related technical jargon, licenses, and degrees are among the other opportunities you will have to come up with keywords to add to your electronic resume. If you are posting you resume on the Internet, look for the categories that website uses and make sure you use them too. Be sure the words "administrative assistant" appear somewhere on your resume, and use accepted professional jargon, such as "M&A" for "mergers & acquisitions."

The keywords you incorporate into your resume should support or be relevant to your job objective. Some of the best places within your resume to incorporate keywords are when listing:

► job titles
► responsibilities
► accomplishments
► skills

An excellent resource for helping you select the best keywords to use within your electronic resume is the *Occupational Outlook Handbook* (published by the U.S. Department of Labor). This publication is available, free of charge, online at http://stats.bls.gov/oco/oco1000.htm. A printed edition can also be found at most public libraries.

The following is a list of skills almost any company or organization—from a Manhattan brokerage firm to a small branch library in Dayton, Ohio—will want in a secretary/administrative assistant, so any that you can include on your resume will give you an edge:

► basic knowledge of computers—ability to use the latest software programs: word processing, databases, and spreadsheets
► good keyboard skills
► ability to compose effective business correspondence and reports
► ability to relay messages accurately orally or in writing, and to give clear instructions to others
► ability to produce accurate and correctly spelled documents from a transcriber
► ability to understand organizational relationships, roles, and functions
► ability to work independently, solve problems, and make decisions
► willingness to take instruction
► ability to take rapid notes and reproduce documents from those notes

- ▶ good telephone skills
- ▶ strong editing and proofreading skills
- ▶ ability to plan business trips and activities

Clarity

No matter how attractive your resume is, it won't do any good if a prospective employer finds it difficult to read. The most important rule of resume writing is: Never send out a resume that contains mistakes. Proofread it several times and use your spell-check. For most people, writing a resume is an ongoing process, so remember to check it over every time you make a change. There is absolutely no excuse for sending out a resume with misspelled words or grammatical errors. After you proofread it, ask one or two friends to read it over too. If you are uncertain about a grammatical construction, for example, change it.

In addition to checking spelling and grammar, you want to make sure that your resume is well written. Resume writing is quite different from other kinds of writing, and it takes practice. For one thing, most resumes don't use complete sentences. You wouldn't write, "As manager of the housewares department, I managed 14 employees and was in charge of ordering $2.5 million worth of merchandise annually." Instead you'd write, "Managed $2.5 million housewares department with 14 employees." Still, all the other rules of grammar apply to writing a resume. Tenses and numbers need to match, and double negatives and other awkward construction are not acceptable.

It is also important to be concise, to help keep your resume at a manageable size, and to make important information stand out. In the two examples in the above paragraph, the first requires 23 words; the second, just eight. They convey the same information, but the second does it more efficiently. By being concise and demonstrating good word choice, you highlight the fact that you have skills that are valued highly by employers. The abilities to communicate and organize information well are vital to your future job success, and both can easily be reflected in your resume.

You demonstrate your communication abilities not only by making sure everything is spelled correctly and is grammatically accurate, but also by how well you write your resume. Word choice contributes to the clarity and persuasiveness of your resume. Experts have long recommended using verbs (action words) rather than nouns to promote yourself in a resume. Compare "managed $2.5 million housewares department with 14 employees" to "manager of housewares department." The first sounds much more impressive.

However, there is now one caveat to the verb preference rule. As we discussed above, computer resumes, whether scanned or e-mailed, are searched using keywords. These words tend to be *nouns* rather than verbs. So, when writing this type of resume, follow the keyword guidelines spelled out on page 129. For example, a computer would probably find phrases like "data entry" and "word processing," but might not necessarily pick up on "entered information into database" or "typed documents."

Concentration

Each time you send out a resume, whether in response to an ad, following up a networking lead, or even a cold contact, you should concentrate on tailoring your approach for the employer you are contacting. This means having more than one resume, or reconfiguring your resume before printing it so that it conforms better to the job opening for which you're applying. For instance, if you're interested in work as a legal secretary, but you have work experience that you enjoyed at an insurance firm, you're looking first for a position in insurance litigation. But, you might also be willing to take a position in the human resources office of an insurance company or anywhere in a large firm that does insurance work, just to get your foot in the door. Insurance litigation is your dream job; the others are your next choices. To apply for all of these jobs, you will need to alter your resume at least three times.

The resume for the insurance litigation job will stress your prior work experience, the legal secretarial skills you learned at your internship, and how well you did in legal classes at school. Although it depends on the format you are using, you may very well stress them in that order. For a litigation position in a large firm that handles insurance, you'd probably stress your internship and education—but make sure your insurance experience stands out too. For the human resources job, you'd emphasize your insurance experience, basic coursework, and office experience. Finally, for the basic entry-level job, you would want to construct your resume to show that you have solid skills that can be used anywhere.

Earlier in this chapter, you filled out a questionnaire that helped gather the information you need to write your resume. By keeping it close at hand, it won't be that difficult to construct a resume that targets a particular job by concentrating your information so that a prospective employer will see that you are a likely candidate for this opening. In many cases, a few changes to a basic resume are enough to make it appropriate for a particular job opening.

A good way to tailor your resume for a particular opening is to imagine what the job would be like. Imagine, based on the description of the job, the major things you will be expected to do day to day. Then look at your experience and education and decide how to present your information so that the employer will know that you are capable of doing those tasks.

Finally, make sure you get your resume to the appropriate person in the appropriate way. If you got the person's name through a networking contact, your contact may deliver it or suggest that you deliver it in person; most likely, though, you should mail it. If you are making a cold contact—that is, if you are contacting a firm that you found through your research but that is not actively looking to fill a position—make sure you find out the name of the head of the human resources department, or whoever else is doing the hiring, and send your resume to that person. If you are responding to an ad, make sure you do what the ad says. If it directs you to fax your resume, do so. If it asks for a writing sample, make sure you include one. (If you are using a sample you wrote on a job or internship, you must black out all names and any other identifying information.) Demonstrate your ability to attend to detail.

Avoid Making These Common Resume Errors

Stretching the truth. A growing number of employers are verifying all resume information. If you're caught lying, you won't be offered a job, or you could be fired later if it's discovered that you weren't truthful.

Including any references to money. This includes past salaries or how much you're looking to earn within your resume and cover letter, unless the ad you're answering specifically requests your salary requirements or salary history.

Including the reasons why you stopped working for an employer, switched jobs, or are currently looking for a new job. Do not include a line in your resume saying, "Unemployed" or "Out of Work" along with the corresponding dates in order to fill a time gap.

Having a typo or grammatical error in a resume. If you refuse to take the time necessary to proofread your resume, why should an employer assume you take the time needed to do your job properly if you're hired?

Using long paragraphs to describe past work experience. Consider using a bulleted list instead, which highlights important information. Remember that most employers will spend less than one minute initially reading a resume.

Sample resumes are included here to illustrate the different styles. The first is a chronological resume, which highlights previous experience rather than education. The second is a skills resume; this applicant has many of the skills necessary for the position for which he is applying, but no direct experience. The third resume sample—note the form—is designed to be scanned.

Corina Weeble

76 Round Street, Apt. 10

Kansas City, MO 64112

816-555-3944

JOB OBJECTIVE: Administrative assistant in veterinarian's office

QUALIFICATIONS AND SKILLS

• Two years of office support experience and customer relations experience in pet grooming office

• Familiar with Windows 98 and Microsoft Office 2000

• Excellent time-management and organizational skills

• Excellent written and verbal communications skills

• Dependable and self-motivated

• Warm, affectionate manner with animals

EXPERIENCE

1999–present

Paws 'n' Claws Pet Boutique

96 Rosemary Lane

Columbia, MO 65203

Administrative assistant to owner

• Maintained files and records, did light bookkeeping

• Occasionally assisted owner and groomers with animals

• Handled scheduling of all in-town and out-of-town business meetings and grooming demonstrations

• Composed and typed all correspondence

1997–1999

Bob's Friendly Taxi

9 Seymore Place

Iberia, MO 65000

Dispatcher

• Dispatched for three drivers, part-time while in high school

• Maintained schedules and time sheets

• Answered phone, relayed messages to owner

Hamid Al-Jurf, CPS

1916 Papaya Way

Iowa City, IA 52245

319-555-1212

JOB OBJECTIVE: Administrative assistant in a physician's office, with patient contact

QUALIFICATIONS

• Eight years of experience as medical transcriptionist in large teaching hospital

• Two years of experience as ward clerk on inpatient neurology ward

• Sound knowledge of medical terminology in the areas of internal medicine and neurology

• Skilled at transcribing from wide variety of dictating and handwriting styles

• Familiar with Windows 3x, Windows 95, Macintosh plus variety of word processing, database, and spreadsheet software

• Excellent keyboarding skills

• Excellent writing and editing skills

• Excellent interpersonal skills

• Consistently earned outstanding employment evaluations

• Earned Certified Professional Secretary (CPS) rating, 2000

PROFESSIONAL EXPERIENCE

• Transcribed medical records from dictation and handwritten copy

• Trained other medical transcriptionists regularly for six years

• Wrote manual for physicians on how to dictate medical records clearly and effectively

• Set up computer time-keeping method for 20 medical transcriptionists

• Did computer software troubleshooting on night shift for two years

• Had extensive patient contact while a ward clerk on inpatient neurology unit

EMPLOYMENT HISTORY

2000–present   Medical transcriptionist, University of Iowa Hospitals & Clinics, Iowa City

1997–2000   Ward clerk on Inpatient Neurology Unit, University of Iowa Hospitals & Clinics, Iowa City

EDUCATION AND PROFESSIONAL AFFILIATIONS

• Associate degree, Medical Secretary Program, Hamilton College, Des Moines, Iowa

• Bachelor's degree, General Studies, the University of Iowa, Iowa City

• Member of the International Association of Administrative Professionals

Tanya Jacobs, CPS

1450 Dinwiddy Court

San Diego, CA 94555

Telephone: 415-555-9876

OBJECTIVE

Administrative assistant—responsible position as assistant to upper management in travel agency

KEYWORDS

Microsoft Windows, Excel, Lotus 1-2-3, keyboarding, friendly, energetic, self-motivated, composition expertise, Spanish fluency

SKILLS

- proficient in Microsoft Word for Windows, Excel, Lotus 1-2-3
- excellent keyboarding skills—fast and accurate
- experienced in customer relations and service—friendly, professional, personable
- excellent written and verbal communication skills
- self-motivated, independent worker
- ability to work well under pressure
- bilingual—fluent in English and Spanish

PROFESSIONAL HIGHLIGHTS

Wagons West Travel, Denver, Colorado, 1999–present

Administrative assistant

Duties

- keyboarding itineraries
- composing and editing correspondence for three travel agents
- proofreading and editing agency newsletter
- answering phones for six people
- maintaining alphabetic and numeric files

Alfred E. Packer Restaurant & Lounge, Boulder, Colorado

Part-time administrative assistant while in college

Duties

- acted as secretary to the manager
- keyboarding correspondence
- keyboarding menus
- answering phone for manager
- maintaining alphabetic files

WRITING COVER LETTERS

Never send out a resume without a cover letter. The cover letter aims your resume directly at the available job; your resume, in turn, describes in detail why you are the person for the job. If your cover letter is a failure, your resume may not be looked at all. Your cover letter should give the impression that you may be a good candidate for the job. The four elements of the resume—composition, clarity, content, and concentration—apply to cover letters as well. However, because the cover letter has a different function, these elements have some different functions as well.

Composition

Your cover letter needs to grab the attention of the reader, while remaining within the conservative guidelines discussed earlier. As with your resume, avoid fancy fonts and stationery; choose something that matches with your resume. Your cover letter should always be printed on good paper, on letterhead with your name, address, phone and fax numbers, and e-mail address. Letterhead stationery can be done on your computer rather than ordered through a printing company.

A cover letter should be composed as you would a business letter. It should include your address (preferably in the letterhead), the date, the name and address of the person the letter is to be sent to, and a salutation. At the end of the body of the letter, include a closing (such as "Sincerely"), your signature, and your name typed out below. You may use block paragraphs or choose to indent them. It is acceptable to type "enc." at the bottom, indicating there is material (your resume) enclosed with the letter.

Rarely do you need a cover letter that is more than one page. On occasion, an advertisement for a job will ask for a resume and a detailed statement of interest (or words to that effect). Sometimes ads will even ask you to address specific questions or issues in your letter, such as your goals or what you can contribute to the organization. In such cases, you may need to write a letter that is more than one page. Normally, however, you can say all that is necessary in one page.

Clarity

As with your resume, never send out a cover letter with a grammatical or spelling error. Even when you are pressed for time and rushing to get a letter out, make sure to spell-check it and proofread it carefully. Ask someone else to look it over as well. Your letter should be accurate, clear, and concise. It serves as a letter of introduction, an extension of your "advertisement," and needs to convince a prospective employer that you should be interviewed for the position.

Begin your cover letter with an introduction, followed by an explanation of why you are right for this job, and end with a closing paragraph. As with your resume, it is vital that your cover letter be well written; however, it requires a different writing style. Sentence fragments don't work in a cover letter.

While a resume offers a somewhat formal presentation of your background, a cover letter should let some of your personality come through. View it as your first chance to speak with a prospective employer. The resume tells employers what you know and what you can do; the cover letter should tell them a little bit about who you are. However, even though it is somewhat less formal, don't use a conversational tone. For example, don't use contractions or slang.

Content and Concentration

While it is important that your resume be tailored to specific job openings, it's even more important to target your cover letter. In fact, its major component should be its concentration on the particular job opening for which you're applying. Because it is so specific, you will need to write a new cover letter every time you send out your resume. It should never read like a form letter, nor should just repeat the information in your resume. It tells the prospective employer why you are the one for the job.

In the first paragraph, indicate why you are writing the letter at this time. You may write something like:

▶ "I would like to apply for the administrative assistant position advertised in the Sunday *Post*."

▶ "I am writing in response to your ad in the Sunday *Times*."

▶ "I am interested in obtaining an entry-level position with your company."

▶ "We met last July at the NAESAA Convention. I will be graduating from my office technology training program in May."

The first paragraph also usually indicates that your resume is enclosed for consideration, although this may also be in the closing paragraph.

In the body of the letter, you want to explain why your training and experience make you the right person for the job. Highlight and summarize the information in your resume, and take advantage of the opportunity to include more about yourself and your skills. For example, life experience that can't be easily incorporated into a resume can smoothly find its way into your cover letter. For example, instead of writing, "Before secretarial school, I worked at The Store for two years, and before that at The Shop for three years," try something like, "I have five years of retail experience in which I interacted with the public on a daily basis." The body of the letter is your opportunity to explain why the employer should care about your experience and training.

You can also include information about how soon you are available for employment or why (if it's the case) you are applying for a job out of town. You may also mention some of the things that you are looking for in a job—if they are either nonnegotiable or flattering to the employer. Make a direct reference to the specific position and organization. Here are some examples:

▶ "I will graduate on May 16 and will be available for employment immediately. A position with your company appeals to me because I understand you do a great deal of insurance underwriting, and this is a field in which I am very interested. In addition, at this time I am looking for part-time employment and I believe you currently have a part-time opening."

▶ "Although my internship was with the County Attorney's Office, I have come to realize that while that work was interesting, I would prefer a position in the private sector that will afford me to call on my real estate experience. I believe your firm is the place for me and I am certain I would be an asset to you."

▶ "As you look at my resume, you will notice that although I am just now completing my education, I offer a background in administration and problem solving. Since your company has recently undergone a major expansion, I believe you would find me a valuable addition to your staff."

Finally, the last paragraph (some people prefer it to be two short paragraphs) should thank the person, make a reference to future contact, and offer to provide further information. Examples of effective closing paragraphs include:

▶ "Thank you for your consideration. Please contact me at the address or phone number above if you need any further information."
▶ "I look forward to meeting you to discuss this job opening."
▶ "Thank you and I look forward to speaking with you in person."
▶ "I would welcome the opportunity to discuss the match between my skills and your needs in more detail. You can contact me at the address or phone number above, except for the week of the 27th, when I will be out of town. Thank you for your time."

Dear Ms. Williams:

I am very interested in applying for the executive assistant position advertised in the Minneapolis Star-Tribune on February 1, 2002.

As you can see from my enclosed resume, I have four years' experience as an administrative assistant with a small design firm. I enjoyed the work very much. I am an organized, detail-oriented person who gets along well with people. I also have excellent computer skills. I feel that these attributes, along with my work experience, qualify me for the position described in your advertisement.

I would greatly appreciate the opportunity for a personal interview. You can reach me at 555-3944.

Thank you for your consideration.

Sincerely,

Michelle Garcia

INTERVIEWING SUCCESSFULLY

The last step in the job search process, and the one that causes the most anxiety among job seekers, is the interview. A face-to-face meeting with your potential employer gives him or her the chance to decide if you are the right person for the job, and you the chance to decide if the job is right for you. While it is normal to be nervous during an interview, there are many things you can do to calm your fears. The most worthwhile thing you can do is gain a solid understanding of the interview process, and your role in it. By carefully reading the information in this section, and following the suggestions made, you will greatly improve your chances for interviewing success.

Be Prepared

Research your potential employer before your interview and be ready to demonstrate your knowledge. Learn about the type of business of a corporation, small firm, or non-profit. If you're interviewing with a government agency, gain an understanding of its workings. The section entitled "Researching the Field" explained many ways to get the information you're looking for. If you have already done your homework, be sure to refamiliarize yourself just before an interview. If not, now is the time to get the research done.

Preparation should also include practice—find someone to act as an interviewer, and have him or her take you through a mock interview. Ask for an honest evaluation of your performance, and work on those areas your mock interviewer feels you can improve.

Act Professionally

Take the interviewing process very seriously. You are entering the professional world, and you want to show that you fit into that environment. Make several extra copies of your resume, letters of recommendation, and your list of references to bring to your interview. You will also want to bring your daily planner, along with your research materials, a pad, and a working pen.

All of this paperwork will fit nicely in a briefcase or portfolio. On your pad, write down the company's name, interviewer's name, address, telephone number, and directions to the location of the interview.

It's very important to be on time for your interview. Allow extra time for traffic and getting lost if the interview is in an unfamiliar location. Schedule your travel time so that you are in the lobby ten minutes before your interview starts. This will give you time to relax before you begin.

Your appearance is the very first thing a potential employer will notice when you arrive for an interview, so make a positive first impression. Be sure that your clothes are free of stains and wrinkles, and your shoes are shined. If you must make a choice, it is better to be overdressed than underdressed. Personal hygiene is also critical; your hair should be neat, and fingernails clean.

On the morning of your interview, read a local newspaper and watch a morning news program so you're aware of the day's news events and will be able to discuss them with the interviewer. Many interviewers like to start off an interview with small talk. You want to be knowledgeable about what's happening in the world around you.

Speak Confidently

Greet your interviewer with a firm handshake and an enthusiastic smile. Speak with confidence throughout your interview and let your answers convey your assumption that you will be offered the job. For example, phrase your questions this way: "What would my typical day consist of?" "How many administrative assistants work here, and what are their areas of expertise?" Answer questions in complete sentences; however, don't ramble on too long answering any one question. Many hiring managers will ask questions that don't have a right or wrong answer; they ask such questions to evaluate your problem-solving skills.

Keep in mind that a potential employer is not allowed to ask you about your marital status, whether you have kids or plan to, your age, your religion, or your race (these kinds of questions may be asked on anonymous affirmative action forms). If you are asked such a question, you can say, "It's illegal for you to ask me that," and then sit silently until the interviewer says something. Or you can say something like, "I don't understand the question; what it is you want to know?" Better yet, figure out why they are asking the question, and address that issue. Then, the answer to "Do you have children?" becomes "If you're asking if I can travel and work overtime, that's generally not a problem."

Here are some general guidelines to follow when answering questions in an interview:

▶ Use complete sentences and proper English.

▶ Don't be evasive, especially if you're asked about negative aspects of your employment history.

▶ Never imply that a question is stupid.

▶ Don't lie or stretch the truth.

▶ Be prepared to answer the same questions multiple times. Make sure your answers are consistent, and never reply, "You've already asked me that."

▶ Never apologize for negative information regarding your past.

▶ Avoid talking down to an interviewer, or making him or her feel less intelligent than you are.

Ask Questions

You usually will be given the opportunity to ask the interviewer questions, so be prepared. Have a list of questions ready in advance. There's much you need to know about the firm to determine if it is a good fit for you. It's not a one-way street—while you are being evaluated, you are also evaluating the company. If you don't ask any questions, the interviewer may think that you aren't interested in the position. Of course, you may ask about almost anything. You may want to know about the kinds of assignments you can expect, whether you will be working for one person or a number of people, who manages administrative assistants and determines their assignments. These are all legitimate questions. You may also have questions about the resources of the company, such as the computers and other technology.

Anticipate the Questions You Will Be Asked

As part of your job interview preparation, think about the types of questions the interviewer will ask. Obviously, since you're applying for a job as an administrative assistant, you should anticipate detailed questions about the skills you possess and the experience you have using those skills.

Spend time developing well thought out, complete, and intelligent answers. Thinking about them, or even writing out answers on paper will be helpful, but what will benefit you the most is actual practice answering interview questions out loud. Stage a mock interview with someone you trust, who will evaluate your responses honestly.

Most of the questions you will be asked will be pretty obvious, but be prepared for an interviewer to ask you a few that are unexpected. By doing this, the interviewer will be able to see how you react and how well you think on your feet.

The following are common interview questions and suggestions on how you can best answer them:

▶ What can you tell me about yourself? (Stress your skills and accomplishments. Avoid talking about your family, hobbies, or topics not relevant to your ability to do the job.)

▶ Why have you chosen to pursue a career as an administrative assistant? (Give specific reasons and examples.)

▶ In your personal or professional life, what has been your greatest failure? What did you learn from that experience? (Be open and honest. Everyone has had some type of failure. Focus on what you learned from the experience and how it helped you to grow as a person.)

▶ Why did you leave your previous job? (Try to put a positive spin on your answer, especially if you were fired for negative reasons. Company downsizing, a company going out of business, or some other reason that was out of your control is a perfectly acceptable answer. Remember, your answer will probably be verified.)

▶ What would you consider to be your biggest accomplishments at your last job? (Talk about what made you a productive employee and valuable asset to your previous employer. Stress that teamwork was involved in achieving your success, and that you work well with others.)

▶ In college, I see you were a (insert subject) major. Why did you choose (insert subject) as your major? (Explain your interest in the subject matter, where that interest comes from, and how it relates to your current career-related goals.)

▶ What are your long-term goals? (Talk about how you have been following a career path, and where you think this preplanned career path will take you in the future. Describe how you believe the job you're applying for is a logical step forward.)

▶ Why do you think you're the most qualified person to fill this job? (Focus on the positive things that set you apart from the competition. What's unique about you, your skill set, and past experiences? What work-related experience do you have that relates directly to this job?)

▶ What have you heard about our firm that was of interest to you? (Focus on the firm's reputation. Refer to positive publicity, personal recommendations from employees, or published information that caught your attention. This shows you have done your research.)

▶ What else can you tell me about yourself that isn't listed in your resume? (This is yet another opportunity for you to sell yourself to the employer. Take advantage of the opportunity.)

Avoid Common Interview Mistakes

Once you get invited by a potential employer to come in for an interview, do everything within your power to prepare, and avoid the common mistakes often made by applicants. Remember that for every job you apply for, there are probably dozens of other administrative assistants who would like to land that same position.

The following are some of the most common mistakes applicants make while preparing for or participating in job interviews, with tips on how to avoid making these mistakes.

▶ Don't skip steps in your interview preparation. Just because you have been invited for an interview, you can't afford to wing it once you get there. Prior to the interview, spend time doing research about the company, it's products/services and the people you will be meeting with.

▶ Never arrive late for an interview. Arriving even five minutes late for a job interview is equivalent to telling an employer you don't want the job. The day before the interview, drive to the interview location and determine exactly how to get there and how long it takes. On the day of the interview, plan on arriving at least ten minutes early and use the restroom before you begin the actual interview.

▶ Don't neglect your appearance. First impressions are crucial. Make sure your clothing is wrinkle-free and clean, that your hair is well groomed, and that your make-up (if applicable) looks professional. Always dress up for an interview, even if the dress code at the company is casual. Also, be sure to brush your teeth prior to an interview, especially if you have eaten recently.

▶ Prior to an interview, avoid drinking any beverages containing caffeine. Chances are, you will already be nervous about the interview. Drinking coffee or soda won't calm you down.

▶ Don't go into the interview unprepared. Prior to the interview, use your research to compile a list of intelligent questions to ask the employer. These questions can be about the company, its products/ services, its methods of doing business, the job responsibilities of the job you're applying for, etc. When it's time for you to answer questions, always use complete sentences.

▶ Never bring up salary, benefits, or vacation time during the initial interview. Instead, focus on how you (with all of your skills, experience, and education) can become a valuable asset to the company you're interviewing with. Allow the employer to bring up the compensation package to be offered.

▶ Refrain from discussing your past earning history or what you're hoping to earn. An employer typically looks for the best possible employees for the lowest possible price. Let the employer make you an offer first. When asked, tell the interviewer you're looking for a salary/ benefits package that's in line with what's standard in the industry for someone with your qualifications and experience. Try to avoid stating an actual dollar figure.

▶ During the interview, avoid personal topics. There are questions that an employer can't legally ask during an interview situation (or on an

employment application). In addition to these topics, refrain from discussing sex, religion, politics, and any other highly personal topics.

▶ Never insult the interviewer. It's common for an interviewer to ask
what you might perceive to be a stupid or irrelevant question. In some
cases, the interviewer is simply testing to see how you will respond.
Some questions are asked to test your morals or determine your level
of honesty. Other types of questions are used simply to see how you
will react in a tough situation. Try to avoid getting caught up in trick
questions. Never imply that their question is stupid or irrelevant.

▶ Throughout the interview, avoid allowing your body language to get
out of control. For example, if you're someone who taps your foot
when you're nervous, make sure you're aware of your habit so you can
control it in an interview situation.

▶ If your job interview takes place over lunch or dinner, refrain from
drinking alcohol of any kind.

Follow Up

It's a common belief that by conducting a job interview, the interviewer is
simply doing his or her job, which is to fill the position(s) the employer has
available. As a result of this belief, many job seekers show no gratitude to the
interviewer. This is a mistake. Sending a personal and well-thought out note
immediately after an interview will not only keep your name fresh in the hiring manager's mind, but will also show that you have good follow-up skills,
and that you're genuinely interested in the job opportunity.

Individual and personalized thank-you notes should be sent out within 24
hours of your interview to everyone you met with when visiting a potential
employer. Send separate notes containing different messages to each person
you met with, addressing each using the recipient's full name and title. Make
sure you spell names correctly.

Thank-you notes may be typewritten on personal stationery, following a
standard business letter format. A more personal alternative is to write your
thank-you note on a professional looking note card which can be purchased
at any stationery, greeting card or office supply store. The personal touch

will add a lot to further a positive impression and help to separate you from your competition.

Keep your message brief and to the point. Thank the interviewer for taking the time out of his or her busy schedule to meet with you, and for considering you for the job opening available. Make sure you mention the exact position you applied for.

In one or two sentences, highlight the important details discussed in your interview. You want the interviewer to remember you. Don't mention issues under negotiation, such as salary, benefits, concerns, and work schedule. Finally, reaffirm your interest in the position and invite further contact with a closing sentence such as "I look forward to hearing from you soon."

Final Thoughts on Interviewing

There are two more important things to keep in mind while going through interviews. Both will help you to keep not only your interview, but the whole job search process, in perspective. The first is that even if you apply and interview for a job, you don't have to take it. The other is that good interviewers try to sell you on coming to work for them.

Understanding that you aren't required to take a job just because it's offered makes the interview seem less like a life-or-death situation and more like an opportunity to get to know at least one person at the hiring company. You will feel a greater sense of confidence and ease when you keep this in mind. The position you're interviewing for isn't the only one available, so if it feels like a bad fit for you or for them, move on.

Realizing that interviewers should be trying to sell you on coming to work for them is helpful too. A good interviewer has one goal in mind: finding a good person to fill the job opening. They already think you're a possibility, which is why you were invited to interview. Once you're there, it's the interviewer's job to convince you that you would be very happy working at his or her company. Evaluate the information you're given about the work environment; does it fit with what you see and have heard about the firm? Be attuned to the tactics of the interviewer.

EVALUATING A JOB OFFER

You have been offered the job. Now, you have to decide—or perhaps, choose between a number of offers. How should you go about it? First, take some time. The hiring company or organization will not expect you to accept or reject an offer on the spot; you may be given a week or more to make up your mind.

Second, you will need to consider many issues to consider when assessing the offer. This means developing a set of criteria for judging the job offer or offers, whether this is your first job, you're reentering the labor force after a long absence, or you're just planning a change. While determining in advance whether you will like the work may be difficult, the more you find out about it before accepting or rejecting the job offer, the more likely you are to make the right choice. Based on what you learned about the job during your initial research and during your interview, ask yourself the following questions:

▶ Does the work match your interests and make good use of your skills? The duties and responsibilities of the job should have been explained in enough detail during the interview to answer this question.

▶ How important is the job to this company? An explanation of where you fit in the organization and how you are supposed to contribute to its overall objectives should give you an idea of the job's importance.

▶ Were you comfortable with the interviewer or with the supervisor you will have (if you met her or him)?

▶ Is this the kind of atmosphere you would enjoy every day? As you walked through on the way to your interview, or as you were being shown around, did the other employees seem friendly and happy? Did they seem too happy? (If you noticed a party atmosphere, it's possible that not enough is being demanded of them. On the other hand, maybe this is just what you're looking for.) If possible, find out the company's turnover rate, which will indicate how satisfied other employees are with their job and the company.

▶ Does the work require travel? Some secretaries and administrative assistants do travel, with or without their bosses. How would this fit into the way you live your life?

▶ Does the job call for irregular hours? Sometimes this fact isn't advertised. It's best to find out during the interview, then decide if the hours fit in with your preferred lifestyle. Some jobs require night or holiday work; others routinely require overtime to meet deadlines, sales or production goals, or to better serve customers. Consider the effect of work hours on your personal life. Also, depending on the job, you may or may not be exempt from laws requiring the employer to compensate you for overtime. Find out how many hours you will be expected to work each week and whether you receive overtime pay or compensatory time off for working more than the specified number of hours in a week.

▶ What are the opportunities offered by the job? A good job usually offers you the opportunity to learn new skills, to increase your earnings, and to rise to a position of greater authority, responsibility, and prestige. A lack of opportunity for advancement can dampen interest in the work and result in frustration and boredom. The person who offers you the job should give you some idea of promotion possibilities within the organization. What is the next step on the career ladder? Is it a step you'd want to take? If you have to wait for a job to become vacant before you can be promoted, how long is the wait likely to be? Employers have different policies regarding promotion from within the organization. When opportunities for advancement do arise, will you compete with applicants from outside the company? Can you apply for other jobs in the organization, or is mobility limited?

▶ What are the salary and benefits? As noted above, during the interview, it's best to wait for the interviewer to introduce these subjects. And he or she may not! Many companies will not talk about pay until they have decided to hire you. Once they've made the offer, though, they're bound to mention pay, and in order to know if their offer is reasonable, you need a rough estimate of what the job should pay.

To get an idea of what the salary should be, talk to a friend who was recently hired in a similar job. If you have just finished school, ask your teachers and the staff in the college placement office about starting pay for graduates with your qualifications. Scan the classified ads in newspapers and see what salaries are being offered for similar jobs. Detailed data on wages and benefits are also available from the Bureau of Labor Statistics, Division of Occupational Pay and Employee Benefit Levels, 2 Massachusetts Ave. NE., Room 4160, Washington, DC 20212-0001; 202-606-6225. Office-Team, the world's largest administrative staffing service, also offers a free annual salary guide with employment trends, job descriptions, and national salary averages for over 20 administrative positions. You can download a free copy at www.officeteam.com/FreeResources.

If you are considering the salary and benefits for a job in another geographic area, be sure to make allowances for differences in the cost of living, which may be significantly higher in a large metropolitan area than in a smaller city, town, or rural area. Do take into account that the starting salary is just that, the start. Your salary should be reviewed on a regular basis; many organizations do it every 12 months. How much can you expect to earn after one, two, or three or more years? Benefits can also add a lot to your base pay, but they vary widely. Find out exactly what the benefit package includes and how much of the cost you must bear for, say, medical or life insurance.

Finally, there will be an end to the job search process. You will be offered a position that meets your wants and needs, and you will accept it. Chapter 6 details what happens after you begin work, helping you to maximize your potential for success in your new career.

THE INSIDE TRACK

Who: Emily Winters
What: Assistant to the President and CEO
Where: Mills & Medford Academic Publishing

INSIDER'S STORY

I'm the assistant to the president of a publishing company. I do a lot of work that enables him to do his job more effectively; I take dictation and handle correspondence, plan any company parties, handle travel plans, coordinate meetings, and prepare the president's expense report. I also screen all of his incoming calls and make lunch and dinner reservations when necessary.

We are a small company, so I'm also responsible for some of the more general things that keep the office going. I fill the paper trays in the printers, make coffee, order office supplies for all of our departments, and distribute incoming mail and faxes.

Before I had children, I worked as an advertising copywriter. After I became a parent, I got my real estate license. I'd been a full time real estate agent and had done some administrative duties within the office, so when the real estate market went bad, I decided to go with the administrative channel. I work 45 to 50 hours per week at Mills & Medford, but I continue to do freelance writing and still do real estate sales on the weekend.

My qualifications include a good sense of humor, curiosity to find answers for research projects, good phone manners, a willingness to do whatever is needed around the office, a good memory and the ability to anticipate certain needs. It's helpful that I've done all kinds of different work before having this job. People skills have been the most important thing for me, followed by organizational abilities, and writing and computer skills.

CHAPTER six

SUCCEEDING ON THE JOB

In this chapter, you will learn how to succeed once you have landed a job as an administrative assistant. You will find out how to fit into your new work environment, whether you're employed at a large company, retail establishment, hospital, or other work setting. Forming positive relationships with the people you work with and managing your time effectively will also be covered. Finally, a number of other ways in which you can put your career on the fast track, from finding a mentor to handling criticism professionally, will be examined.

CONGRATULATIONS! YOU have worked hard to get the administrative assistant training you need, and you've successfully gone through the job search process. Now, you're employed in your chosen profession. Succeeding in your new position is your next goal. You have an understanding of an administrative assistant's basic duties and how to perform them, but your training didn't cover how to manage work relationships or how to acclimate yourself to a new work environment. There is much to learn regarding how to perform well on the job, beyond what you were taught in the classroom. Many of these topics are covered, including finding and learning from a mentor. When you finish this chapter, you will be armed with the knowledge you need to succeed.

FITTING INTO THE WORKPLACE CULTURE

As an administrative assistant, you may find employment with any number of types of businesses, from international corporations to medical or legal offices to small family-owned operations. Obviously, the workplace cultures of these employers vary greatly. Even among large companies you will find great differences; one may be formal and stiff, another is relaxed and casual, and yet another lies somewhere in between. While every possible workplace culture will not be described here, there are similarities worth exploring, as well as proven tips for success that you can use no matter where you're employed.

Until you're there for a while, you won't know all that the culture of your workplace entails, but you will learn faster the more attuned you are to it. This should be a primary goal of your first weeks and months on the job; once you gain an understanding of the workplace culture, it will help you succeed in your new career by knowing what's expected of you, and what you can expect in return.

Whether you work in a veterinarian's office or a corporation, begin by observing and imitating. Pay careful attention to the work habits of your coworkers and follow suit. If everyone packs their own lunch and eats in a conference room, do the same. If you never spot a fellow employee making a personal phone call, don't make one yourself. If all of the women in the office wear dresses or suits with skirts, don't try to start a trend by wearing pants. Similarly, if all the men leave their jackets and ties on all day, you should, too. After some time has passed, you will know better which customs and traditions you must follow and which you can deviate from. The following paragraphs look at both the traditional world of business, as well as less formal work settings.

The corporate culture relies on a reporting structure and hierarchy to accomplish defined goals. Many large companies adopt this style simply because they have so many people to deal with. One manager (or president or vice president) cannot talk to everyone in the company all the time about their ideas. Instead, there's a functional reporting system. You might have a president, who has seven vice presidents, who have seven directors, who have seven managers, one of whom you work for.

For employees, the advantage in this type of culture is usually security—job security, the availability of additional training (often company paid), and a good, long-term salary with stock options and other perquisites. The disadvantage is that employees do not have as much freedom as in other places of employment and may have to spend more time writing reports and filling out forms than do those in other workplace cultures. In a highly corporate culture, job titles are clearly defined, there is a predefined path to follow for raises and promotions, and there is little opportunity for an employee to shine outside of their own defined job.

There are many opportunities for administrative assistants in less conservative, more casual work environments, as discussed in detail in Chapter 1. In offices like these, jeans and T-shirts may be appropriate attire. These employers may prefer and even encourage individuals to be themselves, giving them a wide range of responsibilities and expecting them to work independently. They tend to leave tradition behind in pursuit of new and better ways to get the job done. Even so, these office environments have their unwritten rules. As with employment at a large company, you will need to pay careful attention in your first few weeks on the job. Do things similarly to the way the other administrative assistants do until you feel you have got a good working knowledge of the workplace culture.

You may find that after your first week on the job that you don't fit into the workplace culture of your employer. While first impressions are important, you should give yourself some time in your new position before deciding for certain that it isn't working. As previously mentioned, it takes time to understand an office environment, and learn all of its unwritten rules. Give yourself a number of weeks or even months to fully integrate yourself into the culture of your new workplace.

MANAGING WORK RELATIONSHIPS

From the moment you began applying for jobs and participating in job interviews, you were establishing and building on your professional reputation. Your reputation may be defined as what people think of you in terms of your personality, competence, and attitude. This perception contributes greatly to what coworkers, superiors, and anyone else you come into professional contact with might say or think about you.

Your success as an administrative assistant will depend in large part on the business relationships you develop and cultivate. This refers to how you get along with others, particularly those you work with. Making a conscious effort to respect others, and becoming a people person, and team player while on the job will help your career immensely.

Basic Rules

When it comes to building and maintaining professional relationships, some basic rules apply to any workplace.

1. **Sometimes peace is better than justice.** You may be absolutely, 100% sure you are right about a specific situation. Unfortunately, you may have coworkers who doubt you or who flatly disagree with you. This is a common occurrence in the workplace.

   In some situations, you need to assert your position and convince the disbelievers to trust your judgment. Your previous track record and reputation will go a long way in helping to convince people to trust your opinions, ideas, and decisions. However, carefully consider the gravity of the situation before you stick your neck out.

   In other words, in a work environment, choose your battles wisely. For instance, go ahead and argue your position if you can prevent a catastrophe. On the other hand, if you are having a debate about an issue of taste, opinion, or preference, it is advisable to leave the situation alone or accept the decisions of your superiors. It may be appropriate to let your recommendation(s) be known, but do not argue your point relentlessly. Sometimes you will be right and people will not listen to you. Always be open to compromise and be willing to listen to and consider the options and ideas of others.

2. **Don't burn bridges.** If you are in a disagreement, or if you are leaving one employment situation for another, always leave the work relationship on a good note. Keep in mind that your professional reputa-

tion will follow you throughout your career. It will take years to build a positive reputation, but only one mistake could destroy it.

When changing jobs, don't take the opportunity to vent negative thoughts and feelings before you leave. While it might make you feel good in the short term, it will have a detrimental, lasting effect on your career and on people's perception of you. Someone you argued with could become your boss someday or be in a position to help you down the line.

If you wind up acting unprofessionally toward someone, even if you don't ever have contact with that person again, he or she will have contact with many other people and possibly describe you as hard to work with or rude. Your work reputation is very important; don't tarnish it by burning your bridges.

When changing employment situations, do so in a professional manner. There are countless reasons why someone leaves one job to pursue a career with another firm, but to maintain a good reputation within the industry, it's important to act professionally when you actually quit. Getting into a fight with your boss, shouting, "I quit!" and then stomping out of the building forever is never the best way to handle things. Even if you think your boss is incompetent, in the heat of anger never let your negative feelings cause you to act unprofessionally.

Instead, if you get into a major disagreement with your employer, don't make a decision to quit impulsively. Spend a few days thinking about your decision. If you decide it's time to move on, start looking for a new job before actually tendering your resignation with your current employer. As a general rule, even if you're not getting along with your boss or coworkers, it's never a good idea to quit your current job until you have lined up a new one.

Once you have actually landed that new job, be prepared to give your current employer the traditional two weeks notice. Arrange a private meeting with your boss or with the appropriate person within the company, and offer your resignation in person, following it up in writing with a friendly and professional letter. Some people give notice and then use their accumulated vacation or sick days to avoid showing up for work. This is not appropriate behavior. Even if your new employer wants you to start work immediately, they will almost always understand that as a matter of loyalty and professional courtesy, it is necessary for you to stay with your current employer for those two weeks after giving your notice.

During those last two weeks on the job, offer to do whatever you can to maintain a positive relationship with your coworkers and boss, such as offering to train your replacement. Make your exit from the employer as smooth as possible. Purposely causing problems, stealing from the employer, or sabotaging business deals are all actions that are unethical and totally inappropriate. Some firms will request your immediate departure when you quit, and will cut off your computer access and escort you out of the building, especially if you're leaving on a negative note. Prior to quitting, try to determine how past coworkers were treated, so you will know what to expect.

As you actually leave the company for the last time, take with you only your personal belongings and nothing that is considered the company's property. Make a point to return, directly to your boss, your office keys and any company-owned equipment that was in your possession. If possible, for your protection, obtain a written memo stating that everything was returned promptly and in working order.

3. **Keep your work and social lives separate.** You were hired to do a job, not to meet new friends and potential dates. While it's important to be friendly and form positive relationships with the people you work with, you should understand the risks associated with becoming too close. Personal relationships can interfere with your job performance, and your job performance can weaken or destroy a friendship, especially if you are working directly with or for a friend.

The challenges associated with at-work romances can lead to disaster. Not only could you endanger your job performance and the relationship, but you may also set yourself up to lose your job. There are many firms and corporations that frown upon office romances, and some that have strict policies against them. If your coworkers find out about your romance, depending upon where you work, you could end up looking for another job.

Your Boss

Executive and administrative assistants and their bosses have a special relationship that some people have compared to a marriage, and in some cases they spend more time together than most husbands and wives. An excellent relationship is a gift, a bad one a daily nightmare; most fall somewhere in between. Because no two bosses are alike, just as no two assistants are alike, it's impossible to give advice that will cover every situation; however, there are a few rules that you can apply to this important relationship that will make it more rewarding and conflict-free.

According to Kay May, administrative assistant to the executive vice president of American Express Financial Advisors, the most important aspect of a boss–secretary relationship is open communication and trust. She counts herself extremely fortunate to have such a relationship with her boss and credits her 16-year-long, challenging, and satisfying job to this relationship. "It's not something that just happens," Kay says. "Both of you have to work at it.

The following list offers some suggestions to help you start building a cooperative relationship with your boss, providing he or she is motivated in that direction.

▶ *Be as clear as possible about what your boss expects.*
If you don't have a formal, written job description and you feel even minimally comfortable asking for one, do so. It takes some tact to do this; you should start by explaining why you want one. Don't simply say, "I'd like my job description in writing, please." That sounds like a challenge, or as though you're going to be too lazy to do anything that's not in the description. It's best to say something like "If possible, I'd like to get a list of the duties I'll be performing every day. I know it's not possible to describe everything, but I don't want to leave anything undone that I'm responsible for." Ask for this information at the very beginning of your relationship, before any tension has built up, so it won't seem like a challenge to your boss's authority.

▶ *If you don't understand your boss's instructions, ask for clarification.*
You cannot work effectively if you don't know what's expected of you. If instructions for doing a task are unclear, you must ask for further details. Don't be afraid of appearing stupid. Most bosses would prefer that you ask for clarification rather than try to muddle through and make mistakes.

▶ *Be flexible.*
If your boss occasionally asks you to do something that's not in your job description—as long as the demand isn't unethical (dishonest or sexist, for example)—it's best to go ahead and do it. If you're rigid about what you will and won't do, your boss is liable to become rigid too. If she or he consistently expects you to perform tasks outside your job description—things you feel are demeaning, especially—eventually you will have to say, very diplomatically, that you are not comfortable doing them. As to what's demeaning, that's an individual matter. Perhaps you wouldn't be comfortable getting coffee or lunch for your boss every day, but may be happy to do it as a favor once in awhile. On the other hand, if your boss was respectful of you in every other way, you might be willing to work such a chore into your regular schedule.

▶ *Try to think of ways to make your boss look good.*
Remember, from Chapter 1, the qualities Deborah Conger said she would look for in an assistant? One of them was "makes me look good." This may sound silly, but it's really just another aspect of good teamwork. If your boss looks good, you and everyone else on your team look good. And a successful team is a happy team and one whose members keep their jobs.

▶ *Don't go over your boss's head except for the most dire reasons.*
It's not an inviolable rule never to complain about your boss to a higher authority. In cases of actual discrimination or harassment, of course you should go to someone else. But in general it's best to take complaints to your boss first and try to settle the matter privately—give him or her a chance to correct bad behavior or explain policies that seem unreasonable or unclear. This takes courage, but the payoffs are large. You may find there's a reason behind your boss's seemingly unreasonable behavior that you never thought of.

▶ *Understand that your boss has problems too.*

When someone has authority over you, it may be hard to remember that they're just human. They have kids at home who misbehave, cats that need to go to the vet, deadlines to meet, bosses of their own—sometimes difficult ones—overseeing their work. If your boss occasionally acts unreasonable, don't take it personally, as it might have nothing to do with you. Of course, if his or her behavior is consistently abusive, you will have to do something about it—confront the problem or even quit. But occasional mood swings are something we're all entitled to.

The best way to handle demands that aren't horrendous but only annoying—shifting deadlines, for example, or failure to make priorities clear—is to ask your boss for a one-on-one conference to clarify things. If you keep focused during the conference on the needs of the team (rather than on who's top dog—in the office, your boss is), it'll probably go smoothly, and your work life will be more pleasant and rewarding.

Your Coworkers

The important thing to concentrate on is work and the needs of the team. This attitude will help keep you focused and will lessen the impact of the inevitable interpersonal tensions that are part of office life. Remember the rules of good ethics, which apply to every situation:

▶ *Take responsibility for your actions.*

Don't blame the company, your boss, or your coworkers for your mistakes. When you're the one in the wrong, own up to it. In a well-run organization, it's not fatal to admit you have made an error. Conversely, don't grovel or say you're wrong when you don't believe you are.

▶ *Never take credit for another worker's ideas.*

Not only is it unethical, but also chances are that eventually you will be found out.

▶ *Do not violate confidentiality, whether the company's or a coworker's.*

As an executive or administrative assistant, you will likely be privy to company or organization information that is confidential. Similarly, you may—especially if you're in a position of authority—be trusted with a personal confidence. Although you may be tempted, do not violate confidentiality in either case, as you can seriously damage the company or organization for which you work or your relationship to customers, clients or coworkers.

▶ *Refuse to cover up serious wrongdoing.*

While violating legitimate confidentiality is always ill-advised, neither should you cover up serious violations of ethics, whether by coworkers, your boss, or even the company or organization itself. "I was just doing my job" is not an acceptable excuse for ethics violations anymore. If you find yourself working for a boss or company with ethics that seriously violate yours, never use the excuse "I'm just an assistant." Even if you can't bring yourself to blow the whistle (which may be the right thing to do, but can have horrible consequences), at least start looking for another job. You will feel better about yourself and about the world.

▶ *Help others, especially new employees.*

Help your coworkers if they need it. (Of course, don't meddle or step in when you sense your help isn't wanted.) Give new employees extra support. Especially important are the seemingly little things—telling a new assistant or clerk when it's time for coffee breaks, or showing the way to the employee lounge and restrooms. We're all familiar with that sweaty-palmed feeling of the first day of work, even the first weeks of work. Remember what it's like to be new and empathize.

▶ *Be positive about others' achievements.*

Never undermine anyone in your office by devaluing their achievements, even if their achievements seem minor. Don't be afraid that another person will look better than you. In a good workplace, one in which teamwork is valued, there's room for everyone to look good.

▶ *Do not complain to the boss about a coworker's behavior.*

Do not complain to your boss about another person's behavior, except when the matter is extremely serious. Unless the behavior of a coworker is really egregious, try every other avenue to resolve the situation before complaining to your boss. If a coworker is committing infractions that violate important ethical rules (consistent sexist or racist treatment of other employees would be an example) or that violate confidentiality or otherwise damage the company or its customers, of course a complaint is in order. But for lesser matters—especially for interpersonal conflicts—complaints to the boss, reminiscent of tattling in grade school, have a way of backfiring. It's best to talk to the person involved, or, if it's something minor, simply to ignore the behavior.

▶ *Don't engage in gossip.*

Gossip hurts the person being talked about, will inevitably come back to haunt you, and also can make you look like you don't have enough to do.

▶ *If you're put in charge, don't overstep your authority.*

If you're promoted to a position of authority, don't become the kind of boss that others dread, either by overstepping or understepping your authority. It is just as important for supervisors to know exactly what's expected of them as it is for their subordinates. Be certain you have a clear understanding of the limits of authority in your new position.

▶ *When conflicts arise, attack the problem, not the other person.*

If the secretary in the billing department is consistently late getting invoices to you and making you work late, talk to him or her when you can remain calm and focused. Keep the discussion centered on how the problem affects your life and work, not on what a terrible person the other secretary is. Just as you would with your boss, ask for a one-on-one conference, and keep the good of the team uppermost in your mind.

Instead of saying, "It's your responsibility to see the invoices get to me on time. How am I supposed to do my job, anyway? From now on, do it right," say something like, "Could we work something out about the timing of the invoice delivery? My husband/wife (dog/cat/bird) really gets upset with me when I stay late at work." If the other person ignores your request, repeat it at intervals. Chances are you will wear him or her down, or your boss will notice the bad behavior and do something about it.

▶ *Within reasonable limits, let go of the need for control.*

Your peace of mind will suffer if you spend an excessive amount of time trying to control things you can't, such as your boss's or your coworkers' behavior. In your administrative assistant job, you are in the role of a support person, so by definition you won't have the kind of control your boss has. Understand and accept that fact, stay focused on what is within your control, and do the very best job you can.

Risky Business

While you might not think of administrative work as being a risky occupation, the U.S. Bureau of Labor Statistics reported in 1999 that repeated-trauma injuries (from activities like typing) accounted for two-thirds of reported occupational illnesses. These injuries can include carpal tunnel syndrome, nerve problems, and tendon inflammation. For more information on preventing job-related injuries, check out these websites:

- The Typing Injury FAQ (www.tifaq.com) offers information and forums on repetitive stress injuries (RSIs) and ergonomics.
- ErgAerobics (www.ergaerobics.com) are stretches and other exercises you can do at work to help prevent RSIs.
- Arthritis.org provides fact sheets and information on RSIs and muscle problems.

MANAGING YOUR TIME

Next to good relationships with supervisors and coworkers, good time management is probably the most important aspect of any administrative assistant job. Being able to know what needs to be done when, and having the work habits necessary for getting it all done well and on time are crucial to your success.

Daily Work Activities

Practicing good habits when dealing with your daily work activities is essential. You will be expected to perform a variety of tasks, many during the same time period. In order to keep things moving smoothly, and complete your assignments well and on time, remember the following:

1. **Know the requirements of your job and what your boss expects of you.** Define your role and know what you are expected to deliver on a daily basis.

2. **Don't get trapped by interruptions and time wasters.** Every job is subject to time wasters. Sometimes you may get caught up by people who want to chat, or you may fall into the trap of playing computer games or reading the news. It is important to allow yourself a small amount of relaxation throughout the day, but set limits for yourself—such as 15 minutes per day—so it doesn't get out of control. If you work with a social, chatty person, don't let yourself be distracted or interrupted. If you are working on something, let your coworker know that you are busy and can perhaps talk later, during lunch. If you do have time to talk to your coworker, try to steer the conversation to work-related topics. Use the time to learn something new from your coworker rather than just chat.

3. **Keep a day planner.** Identify one place where you write (or type) everything down, whether it is a daily planner, personal digital assistant (PDA), or specialized scheduling software for your computer. This is the number-one secret of those who get nearly everything on their to-do list done, when it needs to be done. It's not that these people have better memories than yours; they are just better organized, and can find the information they need at a glance because they keep it all in one place.

4. **Do a small amount of organization when you arrive at work each morning.** For example, look at your planner and do any small revisions needed. From tasks on your agenda, make a to-do list for the day. If your boss likes to have an informal chat in the morning about the day's work, try to schedule it for first thing.

5. **Set priorities.** Ask yourself which of your tasks for today or for this week is most important, and how much time it will take. Be realistic. This is especially important if your job entails frequent deadlines. In some jobs you may have small, daily deadlines, and in others you may have huge, important deadlines spaced further apart—every two weeks or every month. For a heavily deadline-oriented job, your planner will also need to serve as a kind of task flowchart. All important deadlines should be entered clearly and boldly.

6. **Make use of little chunks of time.** If you have five minutes before lunch and you just finished typing a report, there's no reason you can't start another, even if you won't finish it until after you get back. Or you can do just a small part of some pesky job you hate—file 5 invoices out of a stack of 50. You might make a quick call that's on your to-do list. If you're put on hold during a call, take those moments to straighten things in your desk organizer that have been knocked askew. Do anything except sit there staring blankly at the clock. You will be amazed at what you can accomplish. More important, it will improve your attitude by giving you a feeling of control over the time in your day.

Improving Time Management Skills

If you find that this is an area in which you could improve, begin to do so immediately. Learning time management skills won't add more hours to the work day, but it will allow you to use all of your time more productively, reduce the stress in your life, better focus on what's important, and ultimately get more done faster. If you have decided to use a time management tool such as a computer program or PDA, spend the time necessary to learn how to use it properly. These tools are only as effective as their user, and although it may take a large time investment to get started, it will be well worth it.

Next, over the course of several days, analyze how you spend every minute of your day. Determine what takes up the majority of your time, but diminishes your productivity. Perhaps you experience countless interruptions from coworkers, long telephone calls, you don't have well-defined priorities, your work area is messy and disorganized, you have too much to do and become overwhelmed, or you're constantly forced to participate in unscheduled meetings. As you examine how you spend your day, pinpoint the biggest time-wasters that are keeping your from getting your most important work done.

Take major projects, goals, and objectives and divide them into smaller, more manageable tasks. You will need to incorporate your to-do list into your daily planner, allowing you to schedule your time. Make sure you attempt to complete your high-priority items and tasks early in the day, giving those items your full attention. Also, make sure you list all of your prescheduled appointments in your daily schedule, allowing ample time to get to and from the appointments, and if necessary, prepare for them in advance.

Once you commit to using a time management tool, it's important to remain disciplined, using it continuously until it becomes second nature. Initially, you may have to spend up to 30 minutes per day planning your time and creating your to-do list, but ultimately, you will begin saving up to several hours per day. Learning to better manage your time will boost your productivity, which will ultimately make you more valuable to an employer, putting you in a better position to receive a raise or promotion.

Time for You

When you're at work every day all week long, it becomes difficult to get your *life tasks* done. When you have a family and you're juggling the needs and schedules of a number of people, it can be even more difficult. Just as with your job, the key to getting everything done (with time to spare to relax!) is organization. The following are some tips to help you integrate your job with your life.

▶ Make to-do lists and prioritize the tasks you need to accomplish. Keep a list of things you need to do, buy, return, pick up, and drop off, using the same time management tool employed at work (unless it's a computer program). A day planner or PDA works best. Organize your list according to places you will stop. Keep grocery items on one list, pharmacy items on another, dry cleaning on a third, et cetera. Cross things off the lists when you have finished them so you can see what you have to do at a glance.

▶ Use your lunch hour to run errands at least once a week. Identify resources that are close to your work for things you can do during your lunch hour—doctor, dentist, dry cleaner, shoe repair, car repair, hardware store, and so on.

▶ Use the commute between home and work to take care of other errands, such as stopping at the gas station and the grocery store.

MENTORS

Finding and learning from a mentor should be an essential element in your success. It's probably one of the best ways to continue your education on the job, giving you the kind of insider information not covered during your training. Mentoring can also provide you with a professional coach, someone who sees your job performance and knows ways in which you can improve upon it. A mentor is someone you identify as successful, and with whom you create an informal teacher–student relationship. Enter into the relationship intending to observe your mentor carefully, learning from him or her as much as possible.

Finding a Mentor

You will probably need to actively search for a mentor, unless someone decides to take you under his or her wing and show you the ropes. A mentor can be anyone from another secretary to a human resources manager or a superior. There is no formula for who makes a good mentor; it is not based on title, level of seniority, or years in the field. Instead, the qualities of a good mentor are based on a combination of willingness to be a mentor, level of expertise in a certain area, teaching ability, and attitude.

Begin looking for a mentor within your place of employment, but as a November 1997 article in *Fortune* magazine suggests, you need not limit your search to your own company or organization. A mentor from outside will do just as well, as long as it's someone in the same field and someone you trust. When looking within your place of employment, the article suggests you seek counsel from three kinds of mentors within your place of employment:

▶ a higher-up (but not your boss, or you might be accused of simply currying favor) who can give you informal soundings on what your superiors think of your work

▶ a peer from another area of your place of employment, who can teach you about aspects of the company or organization you do not yet know

▶ a subordinate (if you're in a position of authority as, say, office manager), who can tell you what other subordinates think of your supervisory style

Three Great Ways to Find a Mentor

▨ Join a professional organization. One of the best is the International Association of Administrative Professionals, which has local chapters throughout the United States. (See Appendix A for contact information.)

▨ Court an individual mentor in your place of employment or outside it. Invite that person for coffee or lunch. Be frank—say that you want to succeed in your job and therefore want to know as much about how to do so as possible. Most people like to talk about their work, and most people like to give advice. If the first potential mentor doesn't work out, don't be discouraged; look around for another prospect.

▨ Choose a friend who works in the same or a similar field. Ask that person to meet with you regularly to discuss your job. You might invite him or her to lunch for these meetings, and offer to pay.

When looking for a mentor, keep in mind the following questions:

Who in your firm has a great reputation as a true professional?

Does the potential mentor tackle problems in a reasonable manner until they are resolved?

What is it that people admire about the potential mentor? Do the admirable qualities coincide with your values and goals?

Is he or she strong in areas where you are weak?

When you think you have found someone to be your mentor, spend some time watching that person on the job. You can learn a lot about him or her through observation. When asked a question, does she take the time to help you find the solution, or does she point you toward someone else who can help you? The one who takes the time to help you resolve your question is the better choice for a mentor. Observe your potential mentor when he/she is working on a problem. Does he/she do so in a calm manner? Does the problem get resolved? If so, you may have found a good mentor.

Learning From a Mentor

Once you have entered into a mentoring relationship, intend to learn all you can. While there are no set rules about what a mentor can teach you, there are some specifics that are part of the curriculum in many mentoring relationships. The following is a list of things you may learn from a mentor:

▶ what to expect in your work environment
▶ how to communicate with the chain of command in your company
▶ in-depth knowledge about the technology used by your company
▶ the best administrative assistant magazines, websites, and other resource material
▶ what conferences/classes/training programs you should attend

Once you find someone who seems to be the ideal mentor, don't feel compelled to stick with him or her forever. Career growth may open up possibilities to you in new areas of specialization. If that happens, you will probably want to find additional mentors who can show you the ropes in the new environment. However, any former mentors you can keep as friends may not only help you career-wise, but they can also enrich your life in personal ways.

PROMOTING YOURSELF

There are a number of other things you can do to keep your career moving in a positive direction. You can't wait for opportunities to land in your lap. Rather, you should create them yourself by being proactive; promote yourself in your current position, and/or seek out a promotion to a higher-level job.

Building on Your Reputation

No matter how well you work with others and how organized you are, in the end you will be judged by the product you put out. You want to develop a reputation as someone who gets the job done, correctly and on time. To accomplish this, make sure you know exactly what is expected of you. It doesn't hurt to ask for clarification if you're unsure about how to proceed. Take pride in everything you do, and do it to the best of your ability.

Perhaps most importantly, work toward increasing your abilities. You might decide to take a course in grammar, expository writing, the latest office software, or some other pertinent subject at a local community college. Or, you could join an administrative assistant organization, and get involved at a local level. Actively pursue knowledge, experience, and greater involvement in your career, and in the industry in which you work.

One way to do this is to pursue professional certification. The International Association of Administrative Professionals offers two levels of certification: CPS (Certified Professional Secretary) and CAP (Certified Administrative Professional). Some experience is necessary to take the exams; the requirements vary, but you must generally have between two and four years' experience working in the administrative field, be enrolled in a full-time administrative training program, or both. (Go back to Chapter 1 to review the requirements.)

Both certifications include communication, administration, technology, management, accounting, and economics. The CAP is a more advanced certification; it encompasses the CPS requirements as well as an additional section on organizational planning, which tests critical thinking and the ability to apply managerial concepts.

The IAAP reports that its members who have attained certification earn an average of $2,200 more per year than those who have not, making it a valuable credential financially as well as professionally.

Keeping a Record of Your Work

As your career progresses, find a way to keep track of the work you do. On your calendar or elsewhere, write down when assignments were given, a brief description of the assignments, when and if they were modified, and when you completed them. That way, when your performance is reviewed and your boss says, "I think you were late on X last month," you can look at your records and point out that you were told to put that work aside when another, more pressing, matter came up. It also allows you to chart, both for yourself and your boss, the challenges and responsibilities you have been given and handled well.

Dealing Positively with Criticism

When you receive criticism about your job performance, you need to do three things. The first is to remain calm. You need to hear what is being said, and that is nearly impossible when you're upset. Listen and understand without trying to defend yourself or correcting the person who's critiquing your work.

Second, ask for clarification and concrete help to rectify the situation. If you have been told that the travel accommodations you arranged were unsatisfactory, find out exactly what the problem was. Does your boss have a favorite travel agent or travel website that she would rather you consult next time? Ask for specific information in a nonconfrontational way.

Third, follow any advice given, and ask the person who's critiquing you for help in the future. See if you can find a time when he or she can see how you have been doing things and make specific suggestions for changes. By keeping calm, and responding in a nondefensive, professional manner, you can turn a negative critique into an opportunity for positive growth and change.

Getting Promoted

Once you have been on the job for a while, you may decide that the position you hold isn't as challenging or rewarding as it once was. If you work in a large company, there may be promotion opportunities to seek out. Entry-level administrative jobs can lead to higher-level positions with more responsibility, greater visibility, and better pay. You might apply for an opening to work with a boss who's higher up on the chain of command, or in a department that has a more interesting job to do.

Before you seek out a promotion, consider what it would mean to you both personally and career-wise. Although our culture teaches us that getting ahead by climbing up the ladder to success is the direction we should all take, sometimes it makes more sense to hold onto a job rather than trade it in for something we believe to be better. Legitimate reasons you might want to stay in your current position include:

► Your job is rewarding and stable, and you like your boss and coworkers.

► Your family life or your avocation outside of work is important to you, and you don't want added job responsibilities that might sap your creative energy or your time with those you love.

► You don't yet have the skills you need for the next-level job. (If you lack the skills, however, you can begin work on acquiring them.)

To help decide whether you really want to move to the next level in your company or organization, make a list of pros and cons for comparison. For example:

PROS	CONS
More creative work in new job	More comfort and confidence right in current position
Greater challenge and more responsibility	Less time to spend with family
Higher prestige	More visibility may mean more stress
Higher pay	Longer hours in the office

It may take you days to think about your list. Be honest, and include as many items as you can think of. Examine yourself, your real interests, and your likes and dislikes. Are you trying to get ahead because it is something you feel others expect of you, or it is something you want for yourself? Think about where you want to be five years from now, both vocationally and personally.

If you decide you'd like to seek a promotion, either immediately or in the future, prepare well for this important step in your career. The following suggestions may help:

▶ Research the job in question, and make sure you know that you have the skills to do it.

▶ Plan ahead. Continually upgrade your skills.

▶ Volunteer to take on additional projects.

▶ Do a little extra on the social front. Join your office's softball team or volunteer to help plan a fundraiser or the company picnic.

▶ Network, formally and informally.

▶ Look at bulletin boards for posted jobs to which you might advance. If you find a department you'd like to work in, try to get to know someone in it.

▶ Take an active interest in what the company or organization is doing.

▶ Read the trade journals and the company newsletter. Find out as much as you can about the product the company makes or the kinds of activities the organization sponsors.

When it comes time to ask or apply for a promotion, be sure to understand your company's protocol. If applying in person, don't aggressively demand the job, but be prepared to explain why you're right for it. Your enthusiasm and confidence will show if you have researched the job, know you have the necessary skills, and are excited about taking on the extra responsibility. If you need to apply in writing, use the same care as if you were applying for your first position in the company. Update your resume to include your current job, pointing out the skills and responsibilities you possess that are needed for the new position.

Try to keep the application process low key. There's a possibility you won't get the promotion this time around, for any number of reasons. You don't want to hurt your chances in the future by exhibiting unprofessional behavior, such as complaining about not getting the job. You're still employed, and still have a job to do for your boss and your company. Spend some time quietly figuring out why you weren't promoted; keep your ears open for any news about who got the job and why. If it's appropriate, ask the person making the hiring decision for information about his or her choice. If there is something you can do to improve your chances in the future, begin to take steps to do so now.

MOVING ON

Suppose you decide, after several years (or even months), that your new job isn't all you thought it would be. Or suppose it is, but now you have gained so much skill and knowledge that you have outgrown the position and/or the company you work for. The right career move in these circumstances is to look for a new job.

Carol Wang, an executive assistant with a large Chicago law firm, says that quitting a job that wasn't right for her was one of the best career decisions she's made. After completing an Office Technology certificate program, Carol accepted an administrative position with a small company. She quickly found, however, that she and the company were simply not well suited for each other.

"An administrative position can be very high-pressure, since you are responsible for a lot of the day-to-day operations of the office," Carol says. "It's so important to be patient and know how to be diplomatic with people. But there's no reason to stay in a job where people don't respect the work you do. My coworkers now are much more respectful of my position; they understand that I work with them, and not necessarily *for* them."

Carol began as the office receptionist, later becoming an administrative assistant to several lawyers and finally an executive assistant to one of the firm's partners. Her current employer has paid for her to take classes in Excel and Windows 2000 so that she can keep her skills current. She loves her job, but wouldn't be there today if she hadn't had the courage to get out of a position that did not suit her.

When contemplating a job change, be sure of your reasons, and don't do it often. Keep in mind that your resume will be read by every potential new employer who will want to know why you left prior positions. If you list a number of jobs held over a short period of time, you may appear unreliable, difficult to get along with, or simply immature. But there are legitimate reasons for moving on, including the following:

► You have learned new skills or improved old ones to the point where your current job is no longer challenging.
► You like your job but don't find what your company or organization does very interesting.

▶ There's a subject you have always been fascinated by, and you'd like an administrative assistant position connected with it in some way (for instance, fashion design, police work, politics, law, medicine, or landscaping).

▶ You're moving to a new town.

▶ You dislike your job or the office atmosphere for any one of a variety of reasons (dull work, abusive boss, unethical business practices, or simply lack of anything meaningful in common with your coworkers).

▶ You're pretty sure the company you work for is downsizing, or you sense it's in financial trouble. Don't rely on gossip—make absolutely sure—but sometimes the signs are unmistakable.

If you decide you have sound, legitimate reasons for moving on, refer back to Chapter 5. Much of the advice on landing your first job will work as well for landing your second!

FINAL THOUGHTS

As noted throughout this book, the hiring outlook for administrative assistants is good and it doesn't appear likely to slow down in the future. Demand for skilled support personnel should actually increase, especially in the industries experiencing rapid growth, such as health and legal services, personnel supply, computer and data processing, and management, and public relations.

Not only are there always a great number of job openings, but administrative assistant positions are becoming more advanced, with greater responsibility, increasing use of technology, and a wider range of career directions. Pursue each step toward your new career with diligence, perseverance, and a commitment to excellence, and you will be well on your way to achieving success.

THE INSIDE TRACK

Who: Patricia Mulrane

What: Editorial Assistant

Where: Twayne Publishers

INSIDER'S STORY

I have a bachelor's degree in Print Media. I always wanted to be in the publishing industry but wasn't sure what kind of a job I wanted to have. During my senior year of college, I interned at a children's book publisher and worked closely with the executive assistant to the editor-in-chief. I always thought she had an exciting job. People always came to her first asking permission to see the editor-in-chief—she knew so much about the daily business of her boss. They had a great relationship too, very friendly.

On a daily basis, my primary job is to coordinate the functions of the department so that everything runs smoothly. I take many author request phone calls, process payments for our freelance copyeditors and proofreaders, rotate contracts for signatures of executives, and request payments for our book series. I also write some jacket copy, and get manuscripts ready for launch meetings by checking that all elements are present, such as photos and permissions.

I've been surprised to learn how much people rely on administrative staff. It can either be very gratifying to know someone depends on you that much, or very detrimental, depending on the relationship. My group is fantastic, but there are executives who don't have respect for assistants and their opinions, especially at a meeting. It is also difficult to move up in the same company at times—some people always think of you as an assistant and do not want to promote you to a higher position.

On the other hand, I have worked with some wonderful people that taught me things I will carry throughout my career. The publisher is a very kind woman who always told me how much she appreciated my work and was very respectful of me especially to her bosses and coworkers. That really means a lot. The executive editor gave me many opportunities to do real editorial work and wanted to know what I wanted my next step in publishing to be.

Knowing how to talk to people is the single most vital skill anyone can have. Of course organization (especially in a paper-filled industry such as publishing) and computer skills are very helpful. But when you can talk with ease and confidence to someone it helps problem solving and half your daily battle is won.

I am planning on moving up in this industry, whether it be in editorial or another department. My administrative background has helped me immensely—I've worked with every department at some point, dealt with every aspect of project management, problem solving, and a variety of different people. This experience is essential to any job.

Appendix A

Professional Associations and Agencies

ADMINISTRATIVE/EXECUTIVE ASSISTANTS' PROFESSIONAL ASSOCIATIONS

American Association of Medical Assistants
20 North Wacker Drive, Suite 1575
Chicago, IL 60606-2963
312-899-1500
www.aama-ntl.org

American Society of Corporate Secretaries
521 Fifth Avenue
New York, NY 10175
212-681-2000
Fax 212-681-2005
www.ascs.org

Health Care Executive Assistants of the
    American Hospital Association
1 N. Franklin
Chicago, IL 60606
312-422-3719
Fax 312-422-4579
www.hceaonline.org

International Association of Administrative
    Professionals (formerly Professional
    Secretaries International)
10502 NW Ambassador Drive
P.O. Box 20404
Kansas City, MO 64195-0404
Fax 816-891-9118
www.iaap-hq.org

Legal Secretaries International, Inc.
2805 SW 221 St.
Hillsboro, OR 97123-6617
503-591-5987
www.legalsecretaries.org

National Association of Educational Office
   Professionals
P.O. Box 12619
Wichita, KS 67277-2619
316-942-4822
Fax 316-942-7100
www.naeop.org

National Association of Executive
   Secretaries and Administrative Assistants
900 S. Washington Street, #G13
Falls Church, VA 22046
703-237-8616
Fax 703-533-1153
www.naesaa.com

National Association of Legal Secretaries
   (International)
314 E. 3rd St., Suite 210
Tulsa, OK 74120
918-582-5188
Fax 918-582-5907
www.nals.org

NATIONAL ACCREDITING AGENCIES

Here is a list of national accrediting agencies for you to contact to see if
your chosen school is accredited. You can request a list of schools that each
agency accredits.

Accrediting Commission for Career Schools
   and Colleges of Technology (ACCSCT)
2101 Wilson Boulevard, Suite 302
Arlington, VA 22201
703-247-4212
Fax 703-247-4533
www.accsct.org

Accrediting Council for Independent
   Colleges and Schools (ACICS)
750 First Street NE, Suite 980
Washington, DC 20002-4241
202-336-6780
Fax 202-842-2593
www.acics.org

Distance Education and Training Council
   (DETC)
1601 Eighteenth Street. NW
Washington, DC 20009-2529
202-234-5100
Fax 202-332-1386
www.detc.org

REGIONAL ACCREDITING AGENCIES

Middle States

Middle States Association of Colleges and
   Schools
Commission on Institutions of Higher
   Education
3624 Market Street
Philadelphia, PA 19104-2680
215-662-5606
Fax 215-662-5950
www.msache.org

New England States

New England Association of Schools and
   Colleges
Commission on Institutions of Higher
   Education (NEASC-CIHE)
209 Burlington Road
Bedford, MA 07130-1433
781-271-0022, x313
Fax 781-271-0950
www.neasc.org/cihe

New England Association of Schools and
   Colleges
Commission on Vocational, Technical and
   Career Institution (NEASC-CTCI)
209 Burlington Road
Bedford, MA 01730-1433
781-271-0022, x316
Fax 781-271-0950
www.neasc.org/ctci

North Central States

North Central Association of Colleges and
   Schools
Commission on Institutions of Higher
   Education (NCA)
30 North LaSalle, Suite 2400
Chicago, IL 60602-2504
312-263-0456; 800-621-7440
Fax 312-263-7462
www.ncahihe.org

Northwest States

Northwest Association of Schools and
   Colleges
Commission on Colleges
11130 NE 33rd Place, Suite 120
Bellevue, WA 98004
425-827-2005
Fax 425-827-3395
www.cocnase.org

Southern States

Southern Association of Colleges and
   Schools
Commission on Colleges (SACS)
1866 Southern Lane
Decatur, GA 30033-4097
404-679-4500; 800-248-7701
Fax 404-679-4558
www.sacscoc.org

Western States

Western Association of Schools and
Colleges
Accrediting Commission for Community and
Junior Colleges (WASC-Jr.)
3402 Mendocino Avenue
Santa Rosa, CA 95403-2244
707-569-9177
Fax 707-569-9179
www.accjc.org

Western Association of Schools and
Colleges
Accrediting Commission for Senior Colleges
and Universities (WASC-Sr.)
985 Atlantic Avenue, Suite 100
Alameda, CA 94501
510-632-5000
Fax 510-632-8361
www.wascsenior.org/senior/wascsr.html

FINANCIAL AID FROM STATE HIGHER EDUCATION AGENCIES

You can request information about financial aid from each of the following state higher education agencies and governing boards.

Alabama

Alabama Commission on Higher Education
100 North Union Street
P.O. Box 302000
Montgomery, AL 36130-2000
334-281-1998
Fax 334-242-0268
www.ache.state.al.us

State Department of Education
50 North Ripley Street
P.O. Box 302101
Montgomery, AL 36104
205-242-8082
www.alsde.edu

Alaska

Alaska Commission on Postsecondary
Education
3030 Vintage Boulevard
Juneau, AK 99801-7100
907-465-2962; 800-441-2962
Fax 907-465-5316
www.state.ak.us/acpe

State Department of Education
801 W. 10th Street, Suite 200
Juneau, AK 99801
907-465-2800; fax 907-465-3452
www.educ.state.ak.us

Arizona

Arizona Board of Regents
2020 N. Central Avenue, Suite 230
Phoenix, AZ 85004-4593
602-229-2500
Fax 602-229-2555
www.abor.asu.edu

State Department of Education
1535 West Jefferson Street
Phoenix, AZ 85007
602-542-4361; 800-352-4558
www.ade.state.az.us

Arkansas

Arkansas Department of Higher Education
144 E. Capitol Avenue
Little Rock, AR 72201
501-371-2000
www.arkansashighered.com

Arkansas Department of Education
4 State Capitol Mall, Room 304A
Little Rock, AR 72201-1071
501-682-4474
arkedu.state.ar.us

California

California Student Aid Commission
P.O. Box 419027
Rancho Cordova, CA 95741-9027
916-445-0880; 888-224-7268
Fax 916-526-8002
www.csac.ca.gov

California Department of Education
721 Capitol Mall
Sacramento, CA 95814
916-657-2451
goldmine.cde.ca.gov

Colorado

Colorado Commission on Higher Education
1380 Lawrence Street, Suite 1200
Denver, CO 80204
303-866-2723
Fax 303-866-4266
www.state.co.us/cche_dir/hecche.html

State Department of Education
201 East Colfax Avenue
Denver, CO 80203-1799
303-866-6600
Fax 303-830-0793
www.cde.state.co.us

Connecticut

Connecticut Department of Higher
    Education
61 Woodland Street
Hartford, CT 06105-2326
860-947-1800
Fax 860-947-1310
www.ctdhe.org

Connecticut Department of Education
P.O. Box 2219
Hartford, CT 06145
860-566-5677
www.state.ct.us/sde

Delaware

Delaware Higher Education Commission
820 N. French Street
Wilmington, DE 19801
302-577-3240; 800-292-7935
Fax 302-577-5765
www.doe.state.de.us/high-ed

District of Columbia

Department of Human Services
Office of Postsecondary Education,
    Research, and Assistance
2100 Martin Luther King Jr. Avenue SE,
    Suite 401
Washington, DC 20020
202-727-3685

District of Columbia Public Schools
Division of Student Services
4501 Lee Street NE
Washington, DC 20019
202-724-4934
www.k12.dc.us

Florida

Florida Department of Education
Turlington Building
325 West Gaines Street
Tallahassee, FL 32399-0400
904-487-0649
www.firn.edu/doe

Georgia

Georgia Student Finance Commission
State Loans and Grants Division
Suite 245, 2082 E. Exchange Place
Tucker, GA 30084
404-414-3000
www.gsfc.org

State Department of Education
2054 Twin Towers E., 205 Butler Street
Atlanta, GA 30334-5040
404-656-5812
www.glc.k12.state.ga.us

Hawaii

Hawaii Department of Education
2530 10th Avenue, Room A12
Honolulu, HI 96816
808-733-9103
www.doe.k12.hi.us

Idaho

Idaho Board of Education
P.O. Box 83720
Boise, ID 83720-0037
208-334-2270
www.sde.state.id.us/osbe/board.htm

State Department of Education
650 West State Street
Boise, ID 83720
208-332-6800
www.sde.state.id.us

Illinois

Illinois Student Assistance Commission
1755 Lake Cook Road
Deerfield, IL 60015-5209
708-948-8500
www.isac1.org

Indiana

State Student Assistance Commission of
    Indiana
150 W. Market Street, Suite 500
Indianapolis, IN 46204-2811
317-232-2350; 888-528-4719
Fax 317-232-3260
www.in.gov/ssaci

Indiana Department of Education
Room 229, State House
Indianapolis, IN 46204-2798
317-232-2305
ideanet.doe.state.in.us

Iowa

Iowa College Student Aid Commission
200 10th Street, 4th Floor
Des Moines, IA 50309-2036
515-242-3344
www.state.ia.us/collegeaid

Iowa Department of Education
Grimes State Office Building
Des Moines, IA 50319-0146
515-281-5294
Fax 515-242-5988
www.state.ia.us/educate

Kansas

Kansas Board of Regents
1000 SW Jackson Street, Suite 520
Topeka, KS 66612-1368
785-296-3421
www.kansasregents.org

State Department of Education
Kansas State Education Bldg.
120 E. Tenth Avenue
Topeka, KS 66612-1103
785-296-3201
Fax 785-296-7933
www.ksbe.state.ks.us

Kentucky

Kentucky Higher Education Assistance
    Authority
Suite 102, 1050 U.S. 127 S.
Frankfort, KY 40601-4323
800-928-8926
www.kheaa.com

State Department of Education
500 Mero Street
Frankfort, KY 40601
502-564-4770; 800-533-5372
www.kde.state.ky.us

Louisiana

Louisiana Student Financial Assistance
    Commission
Office of Student Financial Assistance
P.O. Box 91202
Baton Rouge, LA 70821-9202
800-259-5626
www.osfa.state.la.us

State Department of Education
P.O. Box 94064
626 North 4th Street, 12th Floor
Baton Rouge, LA 70804-9064
504-342-2098; 877-453-2721
www.doe.state.la.us

Maine

Finance Authority of Maine
5 Community Drive
P.O. Box 949
Augusta, ME 04333-0949
207-287-3263; 800-228-3734
Fax 207-623-0095
www.famemaine.com/html/education

Maine Department of Education
23 State House Station
Augusta, ME 04333-0023
207-287-5800
Fax 207-287-5900
www.state.me.us/education

Maryland

Maryland Higher Education Commission
Jeffrey Building, 16 Francis Street
Annapolis, MD 21401-1781
410-974-2971
www.mhec.state.md.us

Maryland State Department of Education
200 West Baltimore Street
Baltimore, MD 21201-2595
410-767-0100
www.msde.state.md.us

Massachusetts

Massachusetts Board of Higher Education
One Ashburton Place, Room 1401
Boston, MA 02108
617-727-9420
www.mass.edu

State Department of Education
350 Main Street
Malden, MA 02148-5023
781-338-3300
www.doe.mass.edu

Massachusetts Higher Education
    Information Center
700 Boylston Street
Boston, MA 02116
617-536-0200; 877-332-4348
www.heic.org

Michigan

Michigan Higher Education Assistance
    Authority
Office of Scholarships and Grants
P.O. Box 30462
Lansing, MI 48909-7962
517-373-3394; 877-323-2287
www.mi-studentaid.org

Michigan Department of Education
608 W. Allegan Street, Hannah Building
Lansing, MI 48909
517-373-3324
www.mde.state.mi.us

Minnesota

Minnesota Higher Education Services Office
1450 Energy Park Drive, Suite 350
Saint Paul, MN 55108-5227
651-642-0533; 800-657-3866
Fax 651-642-0675
www.mheso.state.mn.us

Department of Children, Families, and
    Learning
1500 Highway 36 West
Roseville, MN 55113
651-582-8200
www.educ.state.mn.us

Mississippi

Mississippi Postsecondary Education
Financial Assistance Board
3825 Ridgewood Road
Jackson, MS 39211-6453
601-982-6663

State Department of Education
Central High School
P.O. Box 771
359 North West Street
Jackson, MS 39205-0771
601-359-3513
www.mde.k12.ms.us

Missouri

Missouri Coordinating Board for Higher
    Education
3515 Amazonas Drive
Jefferson City, MO 65109-5717
314-751-2361; 800-473-6757
Fax 573-751-6635
www.cbhe.state.mo.us

Missouri State Department of Elementary
    and Secondary Education
P.O. Box 480
Jefferson City 65102-0480
573-751-4212
Fax 573-751-8613
www.dese.state.mo.us

Montana

Montana Higher Education Student
    Assistance Corporation
2500 Broadway
Helena, MT 59620-3104
406-444-6597; 1-800-852-2761 x0606
Fax 406-444-0684
www.mhesac.org

Montana Office of the Commissioner of
    Higher Education
2500 Broadway
P.O. Box 203101
Helena, MT 59620-3101
406-444-6570
Fax 406-444-1469
www.montana.edu/wwwoche

State Office of Public Instruction
P.O. Box 202501
Helena, MT 59620-2501
406-444-3680; 888-231-9393
www.metnet.state.mt.us

Nebraska

Coordinating Commission for Postsecondary
    Education
P.O. Box 95005
Lincoln, NE 68509-5005
402-471-2847
Fax 402-471-2886
www.ccpe.state.ne.us

Nebraska Department of Education
301 Centennial Mall S.
Lincoln, NE 68509-4987
402-471-2295
www.nde.state.ne.us

Nevada

Nevada Department of Education
700 East Fifth Street
Carson City, NV 89701-5096
775-687-9200
Fax 775-687-9101
www.nde.state.nv.us

New Hampshire

New Hampshire Postsecondary Education
    Commission
2 Industrial Park Drive
Concord, NH 03301-8512
603-271-2555
Fax 603-271-2696
www.state.nh.us/postsecondary

State Department of Education
State Office Park South
101 Pleasant Street
Concord, NH 03301
603-271-3494
Fax 603-271-1953
www.state.nh.us/doe

New Jersey

State of New Jersey
20 West State Street
P.O. Box 542
Trenton, NJ 08625-0542
609-292-4310
Fax 609-292-7225; 800-792-8670
www.state.nj.us/highereducation

State Department of Education
225 West State Street
Trenton, NJ 08625-0500
609-984-6409
www.state.nj.us/education

New Mexico

New Mexico Commission on Higher
    Education
1068 Cerrillos Road
Santa Fe, NM 87501-4925
505-827-7383
Fax 505-827-7392
www.nmche.org

State Department of Education
Education Building
300 Don Gaspar
Santa Fe, NM 87501-2786
505-827-6648
www.sde.state.nm.us

New York

New York State Higher Education Services
    Corporation
One Commerce Plaza
Albany, NY 12255
518-473-1574; 888-697-4372
www.hesc.state.ny.us

State Education Department
89 Washington Avenue
Albany, NY 12234
518-474-3852
www.nysed.gov

North Carolina

North Carolina State Education Assistance
    Authority
P.O. Box 14103
Research Triangle Park, NC 27709
919-549-8614
Fax 919-549-8481
www.ncseaa.edu

State Department of Public Instruction
301 N. Wilmington Street
Raleigh, NC 27601
919-807-3300
www.dpi.state.nc.us

North Dakota

North Dakota University System/State Board
   of Higher Education
10th Floor, State Capitol
600 East Boulevard Avenue, Dept. 215
Bismarck, ND 58505-0230
701-328-2960
Fax 701-328-2961
www.ndus.edu/sbhe

State Department of Public Instruction
State Capitol Building, 11th Floor
600 E. Boulevard Avenue, Dept. 201
Bismarck, ND 58505-0164
701-328-2260
Fax 701-328-2461
www.dpi.state.nd.us

Ohio

State Department of Education
25 South Front Street
Columbus, OH 43266-0308
614-466-2761; 877-644-6338
www.ode.state.oh.us

Oklahoma

Oklahoma State Regents for Higher
   Education
655 Research Parkway, Suite 200
Oklahoma City, OK 73104 405-225-9100
Fax 405-225-9230
www.okhighered.org

Oklahoma Guaranteed Student Loan
   Program
P.O. Box 3000
Oklahoma City, OK 73101-3000
405-858-4300
Fax 405-234-4390; 800-247-0420
www.ogslp.org

State Department of Education
Oliver Hodge Memorial Education Building
2500 North Lincoln Boulevard
Oklahoma City, OK 73105-4599
405-521-4122
Fax 405-521-6205
www.sde.state.ok.us

Oregon

Oregon Student Assistance Commission
Suite 100, 1500 Valley River Drive
Eugene, OR 97401-2130
503-687-7400
www.osac.state.or.us

Oregon State System of Higher Education
P.O. Box 3175
Eugene, OR 97403
541-346-5700
www.ous.edu

Oregon Department of Education
255 Capitol Street NE
Salem, OR 97310-0203
503-378-3569
Fax 503-378-2892
www.ode.state.or.us

Pennsylvania

Pennsylvania Higher Education Assistance
   Agency
1200 North Seventh Street
Harrisburg, PA 17102-1444
800-692-7392
www.pheaa.org

Rhode Island

Rhode Island Office of Higher Education
301 Promenade Street
Providence, RI 02908-5748
401-222-2088
Fax 401-222-2545
www.ribghe.org

Rhode Island Higher Education Assistance
  Authority
560 Jefferson Boulevard
Warwick, RI 02886
800-922-9855
Fax 401-736-1100
www.riheaa.org

State Department of Education
225 Westminster Street
Providence, RI 02903
401-222-4600
www.ridoe.net

South Carolina

South Carolina Higher Education Tuition
  Grants Commission
101 Business Park Boulevard, Suite 2100
Columbia, SC 29203-9498
803-896-1120
Fax 803-896-1126
www.sctuitiongrants.com

State Department of Education
1429 Senate Street
Columbia, SC 29201
803-734-8500
www.sde.state.sc.us

South Dakota

Department of Education and Cultural Affairs
700 Governors Drive
Pierre, SD 57501-2291
605-773-3134
www.state.sd.us/deca

South Dakota Board of Regents
306 East Capitol Avenue, Suite 200
Pierre, SD 57501-2409
605-773-3455
www.ris.sdbor.edu

Tennessee

Tennessee Higher Education Commission
404 James Robertson Parkway, Suite 1900
Nashville, TN 37243-0820
615-741-3605
Fax 615-741-6230
www.state.tn.us/thec

State Department of Education
6th Floor, Andrew Johnson Tower
710 James Robertson Parkway
Nashville, TN 37243-0375
615-741-2731
www.state.tn.us/education

Texas

Texas Education Agency
1701 North Congress Avenue
Austin, TX 78701-1494
512-463-9734
www.tea.state.tx.us

Texas Higher Education Coordinating Board
P.O. Box 12788
Austin, TX 78711
512-427-6101; 800-242-3062
www.thecb.state.tx.us

Utah

Utah System of Higher Education
#3 Triad Center, Suite 550
Salt Lake City, UT 84180-1205
801-321-7101
www.utahsbr.edu

Utah State Office of Education
250 East 500 S.
Salt Lake City, UT 84111
801-538-7500
Fax 801-538-7521
www.usoe.k12.ut.us

Vermont

Vermont Student Assistance Corporation
Champlain Mill
P.O. Box 2000
Winooski, VT 05404-2601
802-655-9602; 800-642-3177
Fax 802-654-3765
www.vsac.org

Vermont Department of Education
120 State Street
Montpelier, VT 05620-2501
802-828-3147
Fax 802-828-3140
www.state.vt.us/educ

Virginia

State Council of Higher Education for
   Virginia
James Monroe Building, 101 N. 14th Street
Richmond, VA 23219
804-225-2628
Fax 804 225-2638
www.schev.edu

State Department of Education
P.O. Box 2120
Richmond, VA 23218-2120
800-292-3820
www.pen.k12.va.us

Washington

Washington State Higher Education
   Coordinating Board
P.O. Box 43430
917 Lakeridge Way, SW
Olympia, WA 98504-3430
206-753-7800
www.hecb.wa.gov

State Department of Public Instruction
Old Capitol Building, P.O. Box 47200
Olympia, WA 98504-7200
360-725-6000
www.k12.wa.us

West Virginia

State Department of Education
1900 Kanawha Boulevard East
Charleston, WV 25305
304-558-2691
wvde.state.wv.us

State College and University Systems of
   West Virginia Central Office
1018 Kanawha Boulevard E., Suite 700
Charleston, WV 25301-2827
304-558-2101
Fax 304-558-5719
www.hepc.wvnet.edu

Wisconsin

Higher Educational Aids Board
P.O. Box 7885
Madison, WI 53707-7885
608-267-2206
Fax 608-267-2808
www.heab.state.wi.us

State Department of Public Instruction
125 South Webster Street
P.O. Box 7841
Madison, WI 53707-7814
608-266-3390; 800-541-4563
www.dpi.state.wi.us

Wyoming

Wyoming State Department of Education
Hathaway Building, 2300 Capitol Avenue,
    2nd Floor
Cheyenne, WY 82002-0050
307-777-7675; fax 307-777-6234
www.k12.wy.us/wdehome.html

Wyoming Community College Commission
2020 Carey Avenue, 8th Floor
Cheyenne, WY 82002
307-777-7763
Fax 307-777-6567
www.commission.wcc.edu

Puerto Rico

Council on Higher Education
P.O. Box 19900
San Juan, PR 00910-1900
787-724-7100
www.ces.gobierno.pr

Department of Education
P.O. Box 190759
San Juan, PR 00919-0759
809-759-2000
Fax 809-250-0275

U.S. Department of Education

Students.Gov (Students' Gateway to the
    U.S. Government)
400 Maryland Avenue, SW
ROB-3, Room 4004
Washington, DC 20202-5132
www.students.gov

U.S. Department of Education
Office of Postsecondary Education
1990 K Street, NW
Washington, DC 20006
www.ed.gov/offices/OPE

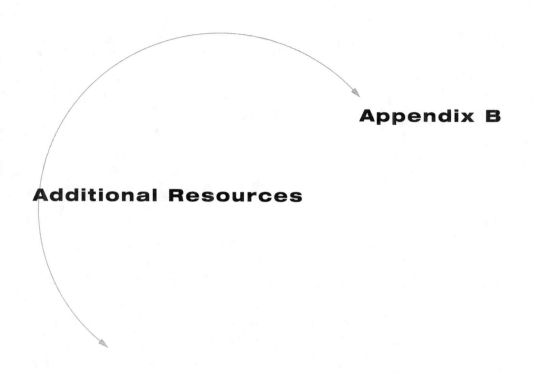

Appendix B

Additional Resources

For additional information on the topics discussed in this book, refer to the following reading lists which are organized by subject, and the list of job-search-related websites.

BUSINESS WRITING

Bartell, Karen H. *American Business English* (Ann Arbor, MI: University of Michigan, 1995).

Chesla, Elizabeth. *Improve Your Writing for Work* (New York: Learning-Express, 1997).

Heller, Bernard. *The 100 Most Difficult Business Letters You'll Ever Have to Write, Fax, or E-Mail* (New York: HarperBusiness, 1994).

Piotrwoski, Maryann V. *Effective Business Writing: A Guide for Those Who Write on the Job* (New York: HarperCollins, 1996).

Stuckey, Marty. *Basics of Business Writing (Worksmart Series)* (New York: Amacom, 1992).

Venolia, Jan. *Better Letters: A Handbook of Business and Personal Correspondence* (Berkeley, CA: Ten Speed Press, 1995).

CAREER RESOURCES

Burke, Michelle. *The Valuable Office Professional* (New York: Amacom, 1996).

Caroselli, Marlene. *Empower Yourself! A Take-Charge Assistant Book* (New York: Amacom, 1997).

Dermott, Brigit, ed. *The Complete Professional: Solutions for Today's Workplace* (New York: LearningExpress, 2000).

Duncan, Melba. *The New Executive Assistant: Advice for Succeeding in Your Career* (New York: McGraw-Hill, 1997).

Jean, Anna-Carin. *The Organizer: Secrets & Systems from the World's Top Executive Assistants* (New York: HarperCollins, 1998).

Lizotte, Ken. *From Secretary Track to Fast Track* (New York: Amacom, 1998).

Spencer, John. *The Professional Secretary's Handbook: Communication Skills* (New York: Barrons, 1997).

———. *The Professional Secretary's Handbook: Management Skills* (New York: Barrons, 1997).

Stroman, James. *Administrative Assistant's and Secretary's Handbook* (New York: Amacom, 1995).

Wisinski, Jerry. *Building a Partnership With Your Boss: A Take-Charge Assistant Book* (New York: Amacom, 1999).

COLLEGES

Chronicle Vocational School Manual: A Directory of Accredited Vocational and Technical Schools 2000-2001 (Moravia, NY: Chronicle Guidance, 2000).

The College Handbook (New York: College Entrance Examination Board, annual).

Peterson's Guide to Distance Learning Programs (Princeton, NJ: Peterson's, annual).

Peterson's Guide to Two-Year Colleges (Princeton, NJ: Peterson's, annual).

COVER LETTERS

Beatty, Richard H. *The Perfect Cover Letter, 2nd Ed.* (New York: John Wiley & Sons, 1997).

Besson, Taunee. *The Wall Street Journal National Business Employment Weekly: Cover Letters. 3rd Ed.* (New York: John Wiley & Sons, 1999).

Enelow, Wendy and Louise Kursmark. *Cover Letter Magic* (Indianapolis, IN: Jist Works, 2000).

Marler, Patty and Jan Bailey Mattia. *Cover Letters Made Easy* (Lincolnwood, IL: NTC Publishing Group, 1995).

Yates, Martin. *Cover Letters That Knock 'Em Dead* (Holbrook, MA: Adams Media Corp., 2000).

FINANCIAL AID

Cassidy, Daniel. *Last Minute College Financing* (Franklin Lakes, NJ: Career Press, 2000).

College Board. *College Costs & Financial Aid Handbook 1999, 19th Ed.* (New York: College Entrance Examination Board, 1998).

Finney, David F. *Financing Your College Degree: A Guide for Adult Students* (New York: College Entrance Examination Board, 1997).

INTERNSHIPS

Anselmi, John, et al. *The Yale Daily News Guide to Internships* (New York: Kaplan, annual).

Hamadeh, Samer and Mark Oldham. *America's Top Internships* (New York: Random House, The Princeton Review, annual).

INTERVIEWS

Bloch, Deborah. *How to Have A Winning Interview* (Lincolnwood, IL: VGM Career Horizons, 1998).

Eyre, Vivian et al. *Great Interview: Successful Strategies for Getting Hired* (New York: LearningExpress, 2000).

Fry, Ron. *101 Great Answers to the Toughest Interview Questions* (Franklin Lakes, NJ: Career Press, 2000).

Medley, H. Anthony. *Sweaty Palms: The Neglected Art of Being Interviewed* (Berkeley, CA: Ten Speed Press, 1992).

JOB HUNTING

Bolles, Richard Nelson. *What Color Is Your Parachute? 2001: A Practical Manual for Job-Hunters and Career-Changers.* (Berkeley: Ten Speed Press, 2000).

Cubbage, Sue and Marcia Williams. *National Job Hotline Directory: The Job Finder's Hot List* (River Forest, IL: Planning/Communications, 1998).

U.S. Department of Labor. *Occupational Outlook Handbook* (Lincolnwood, IL: NTC Publishing Group, annual).

OFFICE POLITICS

Bell, Arthur and Dayle M. Smith. *Winning With Difficult People* (New York: Barron's Business Success Series, 1997).

Dobson, Deborah Singer and Michael Singer Dobson. *Enlightened Office Politics* (New York: Amacom, 2001).

Hawley, Casey Fitts. *100+ Tactics for Office Politics* (New York: Barrons, 2001).

Stone, Florence. *How to Resolve Conflicts at Work: A Take-Charge Assistant Book* (New York: Amacom, 1997).

Tarbell, Shirley. *Office Basics Made Easy* (New York: LearningExpress, 1997).

Wall, Bob. *Working Relationships: The Simple Truth About Getting Along With Friends and Foes at Work* (Palo Alto: Davies-Black, 1999).

REFERENCE

DeVries, Mary. *Prentice Hall's Complete Desk Reference for Office Professionals* (New York: Prentice Hall, 2000).

Dobrian, Joseph. *Business Writing Skills: A Take-Charge Assistant Book* (New York: Amacom, 1997).

Jaderstrom, Susan, ed. *Complete Office Handbook: The Definitive Reference for Today's Electronic Office* (New York: Random House, 1996).

The Professional Secretary's Handbook (New York: Houghton Mifflin, 1995).

Vlamis, Anthony, ed. *Webster's New World Office Professional's Desk Reference* (New York: Hungry Minds, 1999).

PERIODICALS

OfficePro, an award-winning periodical from the International Association of Office Professionals, published eight times per year: www.iaap.org/officepro.

RESUMES

Lefkowitz, Rachel. *Wow! Resumes for Administrative Careers: How to Put Together A Winning Resume* (New York: McGraw-Hill Professional, 1997).

Rich, Jason R. *Great Resume: Get Noticed, Get Hired* (New York: LearningExpress, 2000).

Whitcomb, Susan. *Resume Magic: Trade Secrets of a Professional Resume Writer* (Indianapolis, IN: Jist Works, 1998).

Yates, Martin. *Resumes That Knock 'Em Dead* (Holbrook, MA: Adams Media Corp., 2000).

SCHOLARSHIP GUIDES

Cassidy, Daniel J. *The Scholarship Book: The Complete Guide to Private-Sector Scholarships, Fellowships, Grants, and Loans for the Undergraduate* (New York: Prentice Hall, annual).

Fenner, Susan, et al. *Complete Office Handbook: The Definitive Resource for Today's Electronic Office* (New York: Random House, 1996).

Kaplan, Benjamin. *How to Go to College Almost for Free: The Secrets of Winning Scholarship Money* (New York: HarperResource, 2001).

McKee, Cynthia Ruiz and Philip McKee. *Cash for College: The Ultimate Guide to College Scholarships* (New York: Quill, 1999).

Ragins, Marianne. *Winning Scholarships for College: An Insider's Guide* (Ireland: Owl Books, 1999).

STUDYING

Chesla, Elizabeth and Jim Gish. *Read Better, Remember More, 2nd Ed.* (New York: LearningExpress, 2000).

Wood, Gail. *How to Study* 2nd Ed. (New York: LearningExpress, 2000).

TEST HELP

Cherry, Janet. *Office Systems and Administration: Certified Professional Secretary Self-Study Guides* (New York: Prentice Hall, 1995).

Ehrenhaft, George, et al. *Barron's How to Prepare for the SAT: American College Testing Assessment, 12th Ed.* (New York: Barron's Educational, 2001).

Robinson, Adam, et al. *Cracking the SAT & PSAT* (Princeton, NJ: Princeton Review, annual).

HELPFUL JOB SEARCH WEBSITES

If you have access to the Internet, try checking out these helpful job search sites to find job openings, get career advice, look up salary information, read company profiles, and post your resume for recruiters to read.

Admin-Specific Job Search Sites

Admin-Assistant: www.admin-assistant.com
Admin Connection (specific to Chicago and suburbs):
     www.adminconnection.com
Admin Exchange: www.adminexchange.com
Administrative Resource Network: www.adresnet.com
Health Care Executive Assistants of the AHA: www.hceaonline.org/job.asp
LegalStaff (legal secretaries and general administrative staff):
     www.legalstaff.com
Monster Administrative Support: www.adminsupport.monster.com

General Job Search Sites

CareerSite: www.careersite.com
Federal Jobs Digest: www.jobsfed.com
Headhunter: www.headhunter.net
HotJobs: www.hotjobs.com
Internet Career Connection: www.iccweb.com
Job Bank USA: www.jobbankusa.com
JobSource: www.jobsource.com
USA Jobs: www.usajobs.opm.gov
Wanted Jobs: www.wantedjobs.com

Appendix C

Sample Free Application for Federal Student Aid (FAFSA)

On the following pages you will find a sample FAFSA. Use this to familiarize yourself with the form so that when you apply for federal and state student grants, work-study, and loans, you will know what information you need to have ready. At print this was the most current form, and although the form remains mostly the same from year to year, you should check the FAFSA website (www.fafsa.ed.gov) for the most current information.

2001-2002

The FAFSA

July 1, 2001 — June 30, 2002
Free Application for Federal Student Aid

OMB # 1845-0001

Use this form to apply for federal and state* student grants, work-study, and loans.

Apply over the Internet with **www.fafsa.ed.gov**

 If you are filing a **2000 income tax return,** we recommend that you complete it before filling out this form. However, you do not need to file your income tax return with the IRS before you submit this form.

If you or your family has **unusual circumstances** (such as loss of employment) that might affect your need for student financial aid, submit this form, and then consult with the financial aid office at the college you plan to attend.

You may also use this form to apply for **aid from other sources, such as your state or college.** The deadlines for states (see table to right) or colleges may be as early as January 2001 and may differ. You may be required to complete additional forms. Check with your high school guidance counselor or a financial aid administrator at your college about state and college sources of student aid.

Your answers on this form will be read electronically. Therefore:

- use black ink and fill in ovals completely:
- print clearly in CAPITAL letters and skip a box between words:
- report dollar amounts (such as $12,356.41) like this:

Yes ●   No ⊗ ✓

| I | 5 | | E | L | M | | S | T |

$ | | 1 | 2 | , | 3 | 5 | 6 | **no cents**

Green is for students and purple is for parents.

If you have questions about this application, or for more information on eligibility requirements and the U.S. Department of Education's student aid programs, look on the Internet at **www.ed.gov/studentaid** You can also call 1-800-4FED-AID (1-800-433-3243) seven days a week from 8:00 a.m. through midnight (Eastern time). TTY users may call 1-800-730-8913.

 After you complete this application, make a copy of it for your records. Then **send the original of pages 3 through 6** in the attached envelope or send it to: Federal Student Aid Programs, P.O. Box 4008, Mt. Vernon, IL 62864-8608.

You should submit your application as early as possible, but no earlier than January 1, 2001. We must receive your application **no later than July 1, 2002.** Your school must have your correct, complete information by your last day of enrollment in the 2001-2002 school year.

You should hear from us within four weeks. If you do not, please call 1-800-433-3243 or check on-line at www.fafsa.ed.gov

 Now go to page 3 and begin filling out this form.
Refer to the notes as needed.

STATE AID DEADLINES

AR   April 1, 2001 *(date received)*
AZ   June 30, 2002 *(date received)*
*^ CA   March 2, 2001 *(date postmarked)*
* DC   June 24, 2001 *(date received by state)*
DE   April 15, 2001 *(date received)*
FL   May 15, 2001 *(date processed)*
HI   March 1, 2001
^ IA   July 1, 2001 *(date received)*
IL   First-time applicants – September 30, 2001
     Continuing applicants – July 15, 2001
     (date received)
^ IN   For priority consideration – March 1, 2001
     (date postmarked)
* KS   For priority consideration – April 1, 2001
     (date received)
KY   For priority consideration – March 15, 2001
     (date received)
^ LA   For priority consideration – April 15, 2001
     Final deadline – July 1, 2001
     (date received)
^ MA   For priority consideration – May 1, 2001
     (date received)
MD   March 1, 2001 *(date postmarked)*
ME   May 1, 2001 *(date received)*
MI   High school seniors – February 21, 2001
     College students – March 21, 2001
     (date received)
MN   June 30, 2002 *(date received)*
MO   April 1, 2001 *(date received)*
MT   For priority consideration – March 1, 2001
     (date postmarked)
NC   March 15, 2001 *(date received)*
ND   April 15, 2001 *(date processed)*
NH   May 1, 2001 *(date received)*
^ NJ   June 1, 2001 if you received a
     Tuition Aid Grant in 2000-2001
     All other applicants
     – October 1, 2001, for fall and spring terms
     – March 1, 2002, for spring term only
     (date received)
*^ NY   May 1, 2002 *(date postmarked)*
OH   October 1, 2001 *(date received)*
OK   For priority consideration – April 30, 2001
     Final deadline – June 30, 2001
     (date received)
OR   May 1, 2002 *(date received)*
* PA   All 2000-2001 State Grant recipients and all
     non-2000-2001 State Grant recipients in
     degree programs – May 1, 2001
     All other applicants – August 1, 2001
     (date received)
PR   May 2, 2002 *(date application signed)*
RI   March 1, 2001 *(date received)*
SC   June 30, 2001 *(date received)*
TN   May 1, 2001 *(date processed)*
*^ WV   March 1, 2001 *(date received)*

Check with your financial aid administrator for these states: AK, AL, *AS, *CT, CO, *FM, GA, *GU, ID, *MH, *MP, MS, *NE, *NM, *NV, *PW, *SD, *TX, UT, *VA, *VI, *VT, WA, WI, and *WY.

^ *Applicants encouraged to obtain proof of mailing.*
* *Additional form may be required*

STATE AID DEADLINES

Notes for questions **13–14** (page 3)

If you are an eligible noncitizen, write in your eight or nine digit Alien Registration Number. Generally, you are an eligible noncitizen if you are: (1) a U.S. permanent resident and you have an Alien Registration Receipt Card (I-551); (2) a conditional permanent resident (I-551C); or (3) an other eligible noncitizen with an Arrival-Departure Record (I-94) from the U.S. Immigration and Naturalization Service showing any one of the following designations: "Refugee," "Asylum Granted," "Indefinite Parole," "Humanitarian Parole," or "Cuban-Haitian Entrant." If you are in the U.S. on only an F1 or F2 student visa, or only a J1 or J2 exchange visitor visa, or a G series visa (pertaining to international organizations), you must fill in oval **c**. If you are neither a citizen nor eligible noncitizen, you are not eligible for federal student aid. However, you may be eligible for state or college aid.

Notes for questions **17–21** (page 3)

For undergraduates, full time generally means taking at least 12 credit hours in a term or 24 clock hours per week. 3/4 time generally means taking at least 9 credit hours in a term or 18 clock hours per week. Half time generally means taking at least 6 credit hours in a term or 12 clock hours per week. Provide this information about the college you plan to attend.

Notes for question **29** (page 3) — Enter the correct number in the box in question 29.

Enter **1** for 1st bachelor's degree
Enter **2** for 2nd bachelor's degree
Enter **3** for associate degree (occupational or technical program)
Enter **4** for associate degree (general education or transfer program)
Enter **5** for certificate or diploma for completing an occupational, technical, or educational program of less than two years

Enter **6** for certificate or diploma for completing an occupational, technical, or educational program of at least two years
Enter **7** for teaching credential program (nondegree program)
Enter **8** for graduate or professional degree
Enter **9** for other/undecided

Notes for question **30** (page 3) — Enter the correct number in the box in question 30.

Enter **0** for 1st year undergraduate/never attended college
Enter **1** for 1st year undergraduate/attended college before
Enter **2** for 2nd year undergraduate/sophomore
Enter **3** for 3rd year undergraduate/junior

Enter **4** for 4th year undergraduate/senior
Enter **5** for 5th year/other undergraduate
Enter **6** for 1st year graduate/professional
Enter **7** for continuing graduate/professional or beyond

Notes for questions **37 c. and d.** (page 4) and **71 c. and d.** (page 5)

If you filed or will file a foreign tax return, or a tax return with Puerto Rico, Guam, American Samoa, the Virgin Islands, the Marshall Islands, the Federated States of Micronesia, or Palau, use the information from that return to fill out this form. If you filed a foreign return, convert all figures to U.S. dollars, using the exchange rate that is in effect today.

Notes for questions **38** (page 4) and **72** (page 5)

In general, a person is eligible to file a 1040A or 1040EZ if he or she makes less than $50,000, does not itemize deductions, does not receive income from his or her own business or farm, and does not receive alimony. A person is not eligible if he or she itemizes deductions, receives self-employment income or alimony, or is required to file Schedule D for capital gains.

Notes for questions **41** (page 4) and **75** (page 5) — only for people who filed a 1040EZ or Telefile

On the 1040EZ, if a person answered "Yes" on line 5, use EZ worksheet line F to determine the number of exemptions ($2,800 equals one exemption). If a person answered "No" on line 5, enter 01 if he or she is single, or 02 if he or she is married.

On the Telefile, use line J to determine the number of exemptions ($2,800 equals one exemption).

Notes for questions **47–48** (page 4) and **81–82** (page 5)

Net worth means current value minus debt. If net worth is one million or more, enter $999,999. If net worth is negative, enter 0.

Investments include real estate (do not include the home you live in), trust funds, money market funds, mutual funds, certificates of deposit, stocks, stock options, bonds, other securities, education IRAs, installment and land sale contracts (including mortgages held), commodities, etc. Investment value includes the market value of these investments as of today. Investment debt means only those debts that are related to the investments.

Investments do not include the home you live in, cash, savings, checking accounts, the value of life insurance and retirement plans (pension funds, annuities, noneducation IRAs, Keogh plans, etc.), or the value of prepaid tuition plans.

Business and/or investment farm value includes the market value of land, buildings, machinery, equipment, inventory, etc. Business and/or investment farm debt means only those debts for which the business or investment farm was used as collateral.

Notes for question **58** (page 4)

Answer **"No"** (you are not a veteran) if you (1) have never engaged in active duty in the U.S. Armed Forces, (2) are currently an ROTC student or a cadet or midshipman at a service academy, or (3) are a National Guard or Reserves enlistee activated only for training. Also answer "No" if you are currently serving in the U.S. Armed Forces and will continue to serve through June 30, 2002.

Answer **"Yes"** (you are a veteran) if you (1) have engaged in active duty in the U.S. Armed Forces (Army, Navy, Air Force, Marines, or Coast Guard) or as a member of the National Guard or Reserves who was called to active duty for purposes other than training, or were a cadet or midshipman at one of the service academies, **and** (2) were released under a condition other than dishonorable. Also answer "Yes" if you are not a veteran now but will be one by June 30, 2002.

Step One: For questions 1-34, leave blank any questions that do not apply to you (the student).

1-3. Your full name (as it appears on your Social Security Card)

1. LAST NAME: FOR INFORMATION ONLY
2. FIRST NAME: DO NOT SUBMIT
3. MIDDLE INITIAL

4-7. Your permanent mailing address

4. NUMBER AND STREET (INCLUDE APT. NUMBER)

5. CITY (AND COUNTRY IF NOT U.S.)
6. STATE
7. ZIP CODE

8. Your Social Security Number: XXX – XX – XXXX

9. Your date of birth: / / 19

10. Your permanent telephone number: ( ) –

11-12. Your driver's license number and state (if any)

11. LICENSE NUMBER
12. STATE

13. Are you a U.S. citizen? Pick one. **See Page 2.**
- a. Yes, I am a U.S. citizen. .... ○ 1
- b. No, but I am an eligible noncitizen. **Fill in question 14.** ..... ○ 2
- c. No, I am not a citizen or eligible noncitizen. .... ○ 3

14. ALIEN REGISTRATION NUMBER: A

15. What is your marital status as of today?
- I am single, divorced, or widowed. ○ 1
- I am married/remarried. ○ 2
- I am separated. ○ 3

16. Month and year you were married, separated, divorced, or widowed
MONTH / YEAR

For each question (17 - 21), please mark whether you will be full time, 3/4 time, half time, less than half time, or not attending. **See page 2.**

17. Summer 2001	Full time/Not sure ○ 1	3/4 time ○ 2	Half time ○ 3	Less than half time ○ 4	Not attending ○ 5
18. Fall 2001	Full time/Not sure ○ 1	3/4 time ○ 2	Half time ○ 3	Less than half time ○ 4	Not attending ○ 5
19. Winter 2001-2002	Full time/Not sure ○ 1	3/4 time ○ 2	Half time ○ 3	Less than half time ○ 4	Not attending ○ 5
20. Spring 2002	Full time/Not sure ○ 1	3/4 time ○ 2	Half time ○ 3	Less than half time ○ 4	Not attending ○ 5
21. Summer 2002	Full time/Not sure ○ 1	3/4 time ○ 2	Half time ○ 3	Less than half time ○ 4	Not attending ○ 5

22. Highest school your father completed: Middle school/Jr. High ○ 1 High school ○ 2 College or beyond ○ 3 Other/unknown ○ 4

23. Highest school your mother completed: Middle school/Jr. High ○ 1 High school ○ 2 College or beyond ○ 3 Other/unknown ○ 4

24. What is your state of legal residence? STATE

25. Did you become a legal resident of this state before January 1, 1996? Yes ○ 1 No ○ 2

26. If the answer to question 25 is **"No,"** give month and year you became a legal resident. MONTH / YEAR

27. Are you male? (Most male students must register with Selective Service to get federal aid.) Yes ○ 1 No ○ 2

28. If you are male (age 18-25) and not registered, do you want Selective Service to register you? Yes ○ 1 No ○ 2

29. What degree or certificate will you be working on during 2001-2002? **See page 2** and enter the correct number in the box.

30. What will be your grade level when you begin the 2001-2002 school year? **See page 2** and enter the correct number in the box.

31. Will you have a high school diploma or GED before you enroll? Yes ○ 1 No ○ 2

32. Will you have your first bachelor's degree before July 1, 2001? Yes ○ 1 No ○ 2

33. In addition to grants, are you interested in student loans (which you must pay back)? Yes ○ 1 No ○ 2

34. In addition to grants, are you interested in "work-study" (which you earn through work)? Yes ○ 1 No ○ 2

35. Do not leave this question blank. Have you ever been convicted of possessing or selling illegal drugs? If you have, answer "Yes," complete and submit this application, and we will send you a worksheet in the mail for you to determine if your conviction affects your eligibility for aid.
No ○ 1 Yes ○ 3

DO NOT LEAVE QUESTION 35 BLANK

Step Two:
For questions 36-49, report your (the student's) income and assets. If you are married, report your spouse's income and assets, even if you were not married in 2000. Ignore references to "spouse" if you are currently single, separated, divorced, or widowed.

36. For 2000, have you (the student) completed your IRS income tax return or another tax return listed in **question 37**?

  a. I have already completed my return. ◯ ₁   **b.** I will file, but I have not yet completed my return. ◯ ₂   **c.** I'm not going to file. **(Skip to question 42.)** ◯ ₃

37. What income tax return did you file or will you file for 2000?

  a. IRS 1040 .... ◯ ₁   **d.** A tax return for Puerto Rico, Guam, American Samoa, the Virgin Islands, the
  b. IRS 1040A, 1040EZ, 1040Telefile ...... ◯ ₂   Marshall Islands, the Federated States of Micronesia, or Palau. **See Page 2.** ...... ◯ ₄
  c. A foreign tax return. **See Page 2.** ...... ◯ ₃

38. If you have filed or will file a 1040, were you eligible to file a 1040A or 1040EZ? **See page 2.**   **Yes** ◯ ₁   **No** ◯ ₂   **Don't Know** ◯ ₃

For questions 39-51, if the answer is zero or the question does not apply to you, enter 0.

39. What was your (and spouse's) adjusted gross income for 2000? Adjusted gross income is on IRS Form 1040–line 33; 1040A–line 19; 1040EZ–line 4; or Telefile–line I. $ ☐☐☐ , ☐☐☐

40. Enter the total amount of your (and spouse's) income tax for 2000. Income tax amount is on IRS Form 1040–line 51; 1040A–line 33; 1040EZ–line 10; or Telefile–line K. $ ☐☐☐ , ☐☐☐

41. Enter your (and spouse's) exemptions for 2000. Exemptions are on IRS Form 1040–line 6d or on Form 1040A–line 6d. For Form 1040EZ or Telefile, **see page 2.**   ☐☐

42-43. How much did you (and spouse) earn from working in 2000? Answer this question whether or not you filed a tax return. This information may be on your W-2 forms, or on IRS Form 1040–lines 7 + 12 + 18; 1040A–line 7; or 1040EZ–line 1. Telefilers should use their W-2's.

  You (42) $ ☐☐☐ , ☐☐☐
  Your Spouse (43) $ ☐☐☐ , ☐☐☐

Student (and Spouse) Worksheets (44-46)

44-46. Go to Page 8 and complete the columns on the left of Worksheets A, B, and C. Enter the student (and spouse) totals in questions 44, 45, and 46, respectively. Even though you may have few of the Worksheet items, check each line carefully.

  Worksheet A (44) $ ☐☐☐ , ☐☐☐
  Worksheet B (45) $ ☐☐☐ , ☐☐☐
  Worksheet C (46) $ ☐☐☐ , ☐☐☐

47. As of today, what is the net worth of your (and spouse's) current **investments**? **See page 2.** $ ☐☐☐ , ☐☐☐

48. As of today, what is the net worth of your (and spouse's) current **businesses and/or investment farms**? **See page 2.** Do not include a farm that you live on and operate. $ ☐☐☐ , ☐☐☐

49. As of today, what is your (and spouse's) total current balance of cash, savings, and checking accounts? $ ☐☐☐ , ☐☐☐

50-51. If you receive veterans education benefits, for **how many months** from July 1, 2001 through June 30, 2002 will you receive these benefits, and **what amount** will you receive per month? Do not include your spouse's veterans education benefits.

  Months (50) ☐☐
  Amount (51) $ ☐☐☐

Step Three: Answer all seven questions in this step.

52. Were you born before January 1, 1978? .... **Yes** ◯ ₁   **No** ◯ ₂

53. Will you be working on a master's or doctorate program (such as an MA, MBA, MD, JD, or Ph.D., etc.) during the school year 2001-2002? .... **Yes** ◯ ₁   **No** ◯ ₂

54. As of today, are you married? (Answer "Yes" if you are separated but not divorced.) .... **Yes** ◯ ₁   **No** ◯ ₂

55. Do you have children who receive more than half of their support from you? .... **Yes** ◯ ₁   **No** ◯ ₂

56. Do you have dependents (other than your children or spouse) who live with you and who receive more than half of their support from you, now and through June 30, 2002? .... **Yes** ◯ ₁   **No** ◯ ₂

57. Are you an orphan or ward of the court or were you a ward of the court until age 18? .... **Yes** ◯ ₁   **No** ◯ ₂

58. Are you a veteran of the U.S. Armed Forces? **See page 2.** .... **Yes** ◯ ₁   **No** ◯ ₂

If you (the student) answer "No" to every question in Step Three, go to Step Four.

If you answer "Yes" to any question in Step Three, skip Step Four and go to Step Five.

(If you are a graduate health profession student, your school may require you to complete Step Four even if you answered "Yes" in Step Three.)

Step Four: Complete this step if you (the student) answered "No" to all questions in Step Three.

59. **Go to page 7 to determine who is considered a parent for this step.** What is your parents' marital status as of today?

(Pick one.)   Married/Remarried ○ 1   Single ○ 2   Divorced/Separated ○ 3   Widowed ○ 4

60-63. What are your parents' Social Security Numbers and last names?
If your parent does not have a Social Security Number, enter 000-00-0000

60. FATHER'S/STEPFATHER'S SOCIAL SECURITY NUMBER
`X X X – X X – X X X X`

61. FATHER'S/ STEPFATHER'S LAST NAME
F O R I N F O R M A T I O N O N L Y

62. MOTHER'S/STEPMOTHER'S SOCIAL SECURITY NUMBER
`X X X – X X – X X X X`

63. MOTHER'S/ STEPMOTHER'S LAST NAME
D O N O T S U B M I T

64. **Go to page 7** to determine how many people are in your parents' household.

65. **Go to page 7** to determine how many in question 64 **(exclude your parents)** will be college students between July 1, 2001 and June 30, 2002.

66. What is your parents' state of legal residence?   STATE

67. Did your parents become legal residents of the state in question 66 before January 1, 1996?   Yes ○ 1   No ○ 2

68. If the answer to question 67 is "No," give the month and year legal residency began for the parent who has lived in the state the longest.   MONTH YEAR   /

69. What is the age of your older parent?

70. For 2000, have your parents completed their IRS income tax return or another tax return listed in **question 71**?

  a. My parents have already completed their return. ○ 1
  b. My parents will file, but they have not yet completed their return. ○ 2
  c. My parents are not going to file. **(Skip to question 76.)** ○ 3

71. What income tax return did your parents file or will they file for 2000?

  a. IRS 1040 .... ○ 1
  b. IRS 1040A, 1040EZ, 1040Telefile ..... ○ 2
  c. A foreign tax return. **See Page 2.** ...... ○ 3
  d. A tax return for Puerto Rico, Guam, American Samoa, the Virgin Islands, the Marshall Islands, the Federated States of Micronesia, or Palau. **See Page 2.** .... ○ 4

72. If your parents have filed or will file a 1040, were they eligible to file a 1040A or 1040EZ? **See page 2.**   Yes ○ 1   No ○ 2   Don't Know ○ 3

For questions 73 - 83, if the answer is zero or the question does not apply, enter 0.

73. What was your parents' adjusted gross income for 2000? Adjusted gross income is on IRS Form 1040–line 33; 1040A–line 19; 1040EZ–line 4; or Telefile–line I. $ _ _ _ , _ _ _

74. Enter the total amount of your parents' income tax for 2000. Income tax amount is on IRS Form 1040–line 51; 1040A–line 33; 1040EZ–line 10; or Telefile–line K. $ _ _ _ , _ _ _

75. Enter your parents' exemptions for 2000. Exemptions are on IRS Form 1040–line 6d or on Form 1040A–line 6d. For Form 1040EZ or Telefile, **see page 2.**

76-77. How much did your parents earn from working in 2000? Answer this question whether or not your parents filed a tax return. This information may be on their W-2 forms, or on IRS Form 1040–lines 7 + 12 + 18; 1040A–line 7; or 1040EZ–line 1. Telefilers should use their W-2's.
  Father/Stepfather (76) $ _ _ _ , _ _ _
  Mother/Stepmother (77) $ _ _ _ , _ _ _

Parent Worksheets (78-80)

78-80. Go to Page 8 and complete the columns on the right of Worksheets A, B, and C. Enter the parent totals in questions 78, 79, and 80, respectively. Even though your parents may have few of the Worksheet items, check each line carefully.
  Worksheet A (78) $ _ _ _ , _ _ _
  Worksheet B (79) $ _ _ _ , _ _ _
  Worksheet C (80) $ _ _ _ , _ _ _

81. As of today, what is the net worth of your parents' current **investments**? **See page 2.** $ _ _ _ , _ _ _

82. As of today, what is the net worth of your parents' current **businesses and/or investment farms**? **See page 2.** Do not include a farm that your parents live on and operate. $ _ _ _ , _ _ _

83. As of today, what is your parents' total current balance of cash, savings, and checking accounts? $ _ _ _ , _ _ _

Now go to Step Six.

Step Five: Complete this step only if you (the student) answered "Yes" to any question in Step Three.

84. **Go to page 7** to determine how many people are in your (and your spouse's) household.

85. **Go to page 7** to determine how many in question 84 will be college students between July 1, 2001 and June 30, 2002.

Step Six: Please tell us which schools should receive your information.

For each school (up to six), please provide the federal school code and your housing plans. Look for the federal school codes on the Internet at **www.fafsa.ed.gov**, at your college financial aid office, at your public library, or by asking your high school guidance counselor. If you cannot get the federal school code, write in the complete name, address, city, and state of the college.

86. 1ST FEDERAL SCHOOL CODE OR NAME OF COLLEGE / ADDRESS AND CITY — STATE

87. HOUSING PLANS
- on campus ○ 1
- off campus ○ 2
- with parent ○ 3

88. 2ND FEDERAL SCHOOL CODE OR NAME OF COLLEGE / ADDRESS AND CITY — STATE

89.
- on campus ○ 1
- off campus ○ 2
- with parent ○ 3

90. 3RD FEDERAL SCHOOL CODE OR NAME OF COLLEGE / ADDRESS AND CITY — STATE

91.
- on campus ○ 1
- off campus ○ 2
- with parent ○ 3

92. 4TH FEDERAL SCHOOL CODE OR NAME OF COLLEGE / ADDRESS AND CITY — STATE

93.
- on campus ○ 1
- off campus ○ 2
- with parent ○ 3

94. 5TH FEDERAL SCHOOL CODE OR NAME OF COLLEGE / ADDRESS AND CITY — STATE

95.
- on campus ○ 1
- off campus ○ 2
- with parent ○ 3

96. 6TH FEDERAL SCHOOL CODE OR NAME OF COLLEGE / ADDRESS AND CITY — STATE

97.
- on campus ○ 1
- off campus ○ 2
- with parent ○ 3

Step Seven: Please read, sign, and date.

By signing this application, you agree, if asked, to provide information that will verify the accuracy of your completed form. This information may include your U.S. or state income tax forms. Also, you certify that you (1) will use federal and/or state student financial aid only to pay the cost of attending an institution of higher education, (2) are not in default on a federal student loan or have made satisfactory arrangements to repay it, (3) do not owe money back on a federal student grant or have made satisfactory arrangements to repay it, (4) will notify your school if you default on a federal student loan, and (5) understand that **the Secretary of Education has the authority to verify information reported on this application with the Internal Revenue Service.** If you purposely give false or misleading information, you may be fined $10,000, sent to prison, or both.

98. Date this form was completed.

MONTH / DAY / 2001 ○ or 2002 ○

99. Student signature (Sign in box)

1 **FOR INFORMATION ONLY.**

Parent signature (one parent whose information is provided in Step Four) (Sign in box)

2 **DO NOT SUBMIT.**

If this form was filled out by someone other than you, your spouse, or your parent(s), that person must complete this part.

Preparer's name, firm, and address

100. Preparer's Social Security Number (or 101)

101. Employer ID number (or 100)

102. Preparer's signature and date

1

SCHOOL USE ONLY:
D/O ○ 1

Federal School Code

FAA SIGNATURE

1

MDE USE ONLY:
Special Handle

Page 6

For Help — www.ed.gov/prog_info/SFA/FAFSA

Notes for questions 59–83 (page 5) Step Four: Who is considered a parent in this step?

Read these notes to determine who is considered a parent for purposes of this form. **Answer all questions in Step Four about them**, even if you do not live with them.

If your parents are both living and married to each other, answer the questions about them.

If your parent is widowed or single, answer the questions about that parent. If your widowed parent has remarried as of today, answer the questions about that parent **and** the person whom your parent married (your stepparent).

If your parents have divorced or separated, answer the questions about the parent you lived with more during the past 12 months. (If you did not live with one parent more than the other, give answers about the parent who provided more financial support during the last 12 months, or during the most recent year that you actually received support from a parent.) If this parent has remarried as of today, answer the questions on the rest of this form about that parent **and** the person whom your parent married (your stepparent).

Notes for question 64 (page 5)

Include in your parents' household (see notes, above, for who is considered a parent):
- your parents and yourself, even if you don't live with your parents, and
- your parents' other children if (a) your parents will provide more than half of their support from July 1, 2001 through June 30, 2002 or (b) the children could answer "No" to every question in Step Three, and
- other people if they now live with your parents, your parents provide more than half of their support, and your parents will continue to provide more than half of their support from July 1, 2001 through June 30, 2002.

Notes for questions 65 (page 5) and 85 (page 6)

Always count yourself as a college student. **Do not include your parents.** Include others only if they will attend at least half time in 2001-2002 a program that leads to a college degree or certificate.

Notes for question 84 (page 6)

Include in your (and your spouse's) household:
- yourself (and your spouse, if you have one), and
- your children, if you will provide more than half of their support from July 1, 2001 through June 30, 2002, and
- other people if they now live with you, and you provide more than half of their support, and you will continue to provide more than half of their support from July 1, 2001 through June 30, 2002.

Information on the Privacy Act and use of your Social Security Number

We use the information that you provide on this form to determine if you are eligible to receive federal student financial aid and the amount that you are eligible to receive. Section 483 of the Higher Education Act of 1965, as amended, gives us the authority to ask you and your parents these questions, and to collect the Social Security Numbers of you and your parents.

State and institutional student financial aid programs may also use the information that you provide on this form to determine if you are eligible to receive state and institutional aid and the need that you have for such aid. Therefore, we will disclose the information that you provide on this form to each institution you list in questions 86–97, state agencies in your state of legal residence, and the state agencies of the states in which the colleges that you list in questions 86–97 are located.

If you are applying solely for federal aid, you must answer all of the following questions that apply to you: 1–9, 13–15, 24, 27–28, 31–32, 35, 36–40, 42–49, 52–66, 69–74, 76–85, and 98–99. If you do not answer these questions, you will not receive federal aid.

Without your consent, we may disclose information that you provide to entities under a published "routine use." Under such a routine use, we may disclose information to third parties that we have authorized to assist us in administering the above programs; to other federal agencies under computer matching programs, such as those with the Internal Revenue Service, Social Security Administration, Selective Service System, Immigration and Naturalization Service, and Veterans Administration; to your parents or spouse; and to members of Congress if you ask them to help you with student aid questions.

If the federal government, the U.S. Department of Education, or an employee of the U.S. Department of Education is involved in litigation, we may send information to the Department of Justice, or a court or adjudicative body, if the disclosure is related to financial aid and certain conditions are met. In addition, we may send your information to a foreign, federal, state, or local enforcement agency if the information that you submitted indicates a violation or potential violation of law, for which that agency has jurisdiction for investigation or prosecution. Finally, we may send information regarding a claim that is determined to be valid and overdue to a consumer reporting agency. This information includes identifiers from the record; the amount, status, and history of the claim; and the program under which the claim arose.

State Certification

By submitting this application, you are giving your state financial aid agency permission to verify any statement on this form and to obtain income tax information for all persons required to report income on this form.

The Paperwork Reduction Act of 1995

The Paperwork Reduction Act of 1995 says that no one is required to respond to a collection of information unless it displays a valid OMB control number, which for this form is 1845-0001. The time required to complete this form is estimated to be one hour, including time to review instructions, search data resources, gather the data needed, and complete and review the information collection. If you have comments about this estimate or suggestions for improving this form, please write to: U.S. Department of Education, Washington DC 20202-4651.

We may request additional information from you to ensure efficient application processing operations. We will collect this additional information only as needed and on a voluntary basis.

Worksheets

Do not mail these worksheets in with your application.
Keep these worksheets; your school may ask to see them.

Worksheet A
Calendar Year 2000

For question 44 Student/Spouse		For question 78 Parent(s)
$	Earned income credit from IRS Form 1040–line 60a; 1040A–line 38a; 1040EZ–line 8a; or Telefile–line L	$
$	Additional child tax credit from IRS Form 1040–line 62 or 1040A–line 39	$
$	Welfare benefits, including Temporary Assistance for Needy Families (TANF). Don't include food stamps.	$
$	Social Security benefits received that were not taxed (such as SSI)	$
$	Enter in question 44. Enter in question 78.	$

Worksheet B
Calendar Year 2000

For question 45 Student/Spouse		For question 79 Parent(s)
$	Payments to tax-deferred pension and savings plans (paid directly or withheld from earnings), including amounts reported on the W-2 Form in Box 13, codes D, E, F, G, H, and S	$
$	IRA deductions and payments to self-employed SEP, SIMPLE, and Keogh and other qualified plans from IRS Form 1040–total of lines 23 + 29 or 1040A–line 16	$
$	Child support **received** for all children. Don't include foster care or adoption payments.	$
$	Tax exempt interest income from IRS Form 1040–line 8b or 1040A–line 8b	$
$	Foreign income exclusion from IRS Form 2555–line 43 or 2555EZ–line 18	$
$	Untaxed portions of pensions from IRS Form 1040–lines (15a minus 15b) + (16a minus 16b) or 1040A–lines (11a minus 11b) + (12a minus 12b) excluding rollovers	$
$	Credit for federal tax on special fuels from IRS Form 4136–line 9 – nonfarmers only	$
$	Housing, food, and other living allowances paid to members of the military, clergy, and others (including cash payments and cash value of benefits)	$
$	Veterans noneducation benefits such as Disability, Death Pension, or Dependency & Indemnity Compensation (DIC) and/or VA Educational Work-Study allowances	$
$	Any other untaxed income or benefits not reported elsewhere on Worksheets A and B, such as worker's compensation, untaxed portions of railroad retirement benefits, Black Lung Benefits, Refugee Assistance, etc. **Don't include** student aid, Workforce Investment Act educational benefits, or benefits from flexible spending arrangements, e.g., cafeteria plans.	$
$	Cash **received**, or any money paid on your behalf, not reported elsewhere on this form	XXXXXXXX
$	Enter in question 45. Enter in question 79.	$

Worksheet C
Calendar Year 2000

For question 46 Student/Spouse		For question 80 Parent(s)
$	Education credits (Hope and Lifetime Learning tax credits) from IRS Form 1040–line 46 or 1040A–line 29	$
$	Child support **paid** because of divorce or separation. Do not include support for children in your (or your parents') household, as reported in question 84 (or question 64 for your parents).	$
$	Taxable earnings from Federal Work-Study or other need-based work programs	$
$	Student grant, scholarship, and fellowship aid, including AmeriCorps awards, that was reported to the IRS in your (or your parents') adjusted gross income	$
$	Enter in question 46. Enter in question 80.	$

Page 8